A GARDENER'S GUIDE TO

PERENNIALS

Establish a beautiful border with this fine selection
of herbaceous perennial plants

Filipendula purpurea

Tropaeolum speciosum

A GARDENER'S GUIDE TO

PERENNIALS

Establish a beautiful border with this fine selection
of herbaceous perennial plants

NOËL PROCKTER

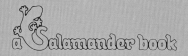

Published by Salamander Books Limited
LONDON

A Salamander Book

Published by Salamander Books Ltd.,
52 Bedford Row,
London WC1R 4LR.

© 1988 Salamander Books Ltd.

ISBN 0 86101 399 9

Distributed by
Hodder and Stoughton Services,
PO Box 6, Mill Road, Dunton Green,
Sevenoaks, Kent TN13 2XX.

All correspondence concerning the
content of this volume should be
addressed to Salamander Books Ltd.

Contents

Text and colour photographs are cross-referenced throughout as follows: 64◗. The plants are arranged in alphabetical order of Latin name. Page numbers in **bold** refer to text entries; those in *italics* refer to photographs.

Credits

Author: Noël J. Prockter is an experienced garden writer. Trained at Kew, he became manager of a leading plant nursery in southern England and then an Assistant Editor of 'Amateur Gardening' magazine. He has contributed to many radio gardening programmes and has authored several books and articles on a wide range of gardening subjects. He is at present Chairman of the Hardy Plant Society of Great Britain.

Editor: Geoff Rogers
Designer: Roger Hyde
Colour reproductions: Rodney Howe Ltd., England
Monochrome: Bantam Litho Ltd., England.
Filmset: SX Composing Ltd., England.

Printed in Belgium by Henri Proost & Cie, Turnhout.

Introduction

What is a perennial plant? All plants are perennials except annuals and biennials. In this book the term perennial indicates herbaceous or hardy herbaceous perennials. This includes hardy plants and some half-hardy ones whose foliage dies back each autumn or winter after flowering and returns to life in the spring, when new young shoots emerge from a clump of dead-looking material. However, perennials are not always deciduous: for example, *Heuchera, Liriope, Geum, Saxifraga* × *urbium* (London pride), *Bergenia* and *Dianthus* have evergreen foliage, and they will provide interest during the winter months.

In this list of 156 plants I have included an occasional biennial, such as *Onopordon acanthium*, the Scotch thistle, which reaches 150-210cm (5-7ft) and seeds itself freely; I also include the sub-shrub perennial *Perovskia atriplicifolia*. Variety is, after all, said to be the spice of life.

Recently I was asked what is meant by a 'wilding'. It is a wild plant, flower or fruit. Some wildings such as *Malva moschata* (Musk mallow) and *Primula vulgaris* (Primrose), are worth a place in our gardens. Other terms might bewilder a beginner.

A *panicle* is a flowerhead with several branches each having a number of stalked flowers. A *truss* is a flower-cluster at the top of a stem, as in phlox. An *umbel* is several stems and flowers arising from a main stem or shoot, shaped like an upturned umbrella. *Deciduous* plants die down or lose their foliage in winter.

Humus is any organic matter, such as leaves, plant stems or animal refuse, when decayed. *Leaf-mould* is decayed or rotted leaves; the best is of oak or beech leaves. Rotted garden *compost* consists of decaying foliage and stems from herbaceous plants, material from the vacuum cleaner bag, kitchen waste, but not potato peelings, as these can grow and produce potatoes. Also, when available, use well-rotted farmyard manure, cow manure, or pig manure; on a heavy clay soil, horse manure is suitable.

General cultivation
As long as you have the strength and will-power to dig, do so. Initial preparation of the soil always pays dividends. When preparing a new bed or border I bastard-trench, ie double dig. To do this take out the

Left: *A beautiful example of a 'classic' herbaceous perennial border. Alive with colour for many months of the year, such a border is a constant delight. Plants of different height, colour and texture have been skilfully blended here to produce a stunning effect. Edging plants along the path give way to subjects of medium height in the centre and these are backed up by tall perennials and shrubs.*

Right: **Lysimachia punctata**
A vigorous perennial that thrives in sunshine or partial shade. 117▶

first spit or two of top soil (a spit is one spade's depth), then fork over the bottom spit of sub-soil and cover with the next one or two top spits. When digging, remove all pernicious weeds such as bindweed, ground elder, docks and dandelions (which my wife calls malignant weeds). Once these irritants are removed, the bed or border has been properly dug with humus incorporated, and the soil has settled, the ground is ready for planting. Always plant firmly and use a hand-fork to make the hole, rather than a trowel. Humus can be well-rotted garden compost, well-rotted farmyard manure or leafmould. Initial preparation is paramount, for once the plants are in the ground there is little one can do; though a gardener I knew mulched all around his plants each year with farmyard manure. Today many gardeners use pulverized bark as a mulch to prevent the soil from drying out during summer, and this also acts as a good weed preventative.

Many plants require ample moisture during hot dry weather. Spray them with clear water in the evening after sunset. Where water has to be applied to the roots of plants, apply a mulch of rotted garden compost or farmyard manure to prevent evaporation.

Stakes and supports

Not all perennials require staking or support; many are sturdy enough to remain upright. But for those that do require some form of support, staking should be carried out at the start of the season, before growth has become too advanced. Peasticks are excellent if inserted in and around the plants or clumps so that the new growth can grow through them; when the plants come into flower the supports are well camouflaged.

Today there are special plant supports for herbaceous border plants; neither sticks nor string is required, just a stout wire stake that supports a galvanized wire ring 20-25cm (8-10in) wide, and the plants grow through them so that the supports become almost invisible. Other types are a triangle with three supports, or a ring with cross pieces and three supports.

Beds and borders
The traditional herbaceous border was planted rather like a shop window, with short, medium and tall plants ranged from front to back. Usually at the back of the border there was a wall, fence or hedge, often a yew hedge. Some gardeners now plant perennials in island beds cut out of a lawn, and this is an ideal method for a small garden because it gets rid of rigid straight lines. Island beds can be round, oval or rectangular. By this method the gardener can get right around the bed.

Choice of plants
Most gardeners have their favourite plants that they wish to grow. Remember that a bed or border can look rather dull during late autumn and winter, and this can be partly avoided by growing a few clumps of plants that retain their foliage throughout the year, such as *Liriope, Saxifraga × urbium* (London pride), *Iberis sempervirens* (Candytuft), *Bergenia, Helleborus, Dianthus, Heuchera, Phlomis russeliana, Sisyrinchium striatum* and *Iris foetidissima.*

To add interest a few shrubs can be included with the herbaceous plants, such as helianthemums, *Ruta graveolens* 'Jackman's Blue', *Rosmarinus* 'Jessop's Upright', *Senecio* 'Sunshine', *Hypericum*

Above: **Rudbeckia fulgida 'Goldsturm'**
Lovely daisy-like blooms on stems up to 60cm (24in) in height. 149▶

Left: *The perfect match of a superb lawn and richly planted borders.*

Above:
Cortaderia selloana 'Pumila'
A lovely compact pampas grass. 55♦

Right:
Anemone 'Honorine Jobert'
Superb for late summer flowers. 22♦

elatum 'Elstead variety', *Lavandula* 'Hidcote Blue', *Hebe pinguifolia* 'Pagei', *Euonymus* 'Emerald 'n Gold', *Berberis thunbergii* 'Aurea'.

When planning a border or island bed, remember that many plants look more effective when planted in groups of three, four or five to the square metre or yard. In a small garden, however, some plants are best grown alone, eg *Aruncus sylvester, Stipa pennata* (a handsome grass), *Cortaderia selloana* 'Pumila' (a dwarf pampas grass).

Propagation

A vast number of perennials can be increased from seed and in many cases the seedling plants will be like their parents. In other instances they will vary in colour: for example, *Lupinus polyphyllus* (the Russell lupin) produces a wide range of colours from one packet of seed. Therefore with many plants it will be necessary to divide them to retain a desirable colour, in either autumn or spring.

Division can be performed in several ways: pull a plant apart with the hands; cut through it with a stout sharp knife; use two hand-forks, placing them back to back, then grip the handles together and ease the plant apart gradually.

Plants such as anchusas and poppies can be increased by taking root cuttings in the autumn or winter months. To do this cut the roots into approximately 3-5cm (1.2-2in) lengths, making a horizontal cut at the top and a slanting cut at the base to avoid inserting the cuttings upside down. Where cuttings are up to 5cm (2in) long, a box will need to be 8cm (3.2in) deep. Fill the box with a mixture of 1 part medium loam, 2 parts granulated peat and 3 parts coarse silver sand (all parts by volume); no fertilizers are required with this mixture. I have used

this mixture many times but if peat has not been available I have used well-rotted oak or beech leaf-mould. Today many growers use soil-less mixture, which is fine; when the cuttings are rooted they can be potted or lined out in a nursery row.

When using peat, make sure it is properly moistened before mixing it with loam and sand; unless it is, water will not be soaked up afterwards. When using pots, boxes or pans, always make certain that they are clean before use, and well crocked, ie place broken pieces of pot and dry leaves in the bottom of the container to ensure good drainage. When using soil-less mixtures, crocks are not necessary, and the mixture must not be made too firm.

Pests and diseases

Perhaps the worst pest – apart from a cat scratching around newly cultivated soil – is the slug, which adores luscious new shoots. Today there are plenty of slug-killers on the market. Snails also do damage, especially to new young shoots. Another very common pest is the greenfly or aphid. To control these, spray or dust with pyrethrum or malathion. The best way to avoid phlox eelworm – a small pest that cannot be seen by the naked eye – is to increase phlox from root cuttings taken from clean stock. Phlox roots are rather like bootlaces. Cut them into 8cm (3.2in) lengths, lay them on cuttings mixture, and cover them. Another pest that often causes havoc is the Solomon's seal sawfly, which disfigures foliage by chewing it to pieces. Control by hand picking, or by spraying with malathion. Ants, too, can be a nuisance; pyrethrum will help to control them, but there are also various specific ant-killers on the market.

**Above: Achillea filipendulina
'Coronation Gold'**
*The pale yellow flowerheads are
borne on stout stems up to 90cm
(3ft) high. Plant in a sheltered spot or
provide adequate support.* 17♦

Left: Acanthus mollis
*Both the flowers and foliage of this
dramatic looking plant are
handsome. A single specimen would
suit a small garden because its roots
can be invasive.* 17♦

**Right: Achillea millefolium
'Cerise Queen'**
*A lovely plant for the front of the
border. The flat flowerheads are
carried on stems 60cm (24in) tall and
may need support.* 18♦

Above: **Aconitum wilsonii**
Up to 180cm (6ft) in height, this stately plant produces striking blue flowers in late summer. Grow in deep fertile soil for best results; keep moist if planted in full sun. 18♦

Left: **Alchemilla mollis**
This adaptable plant is prized by flower arrangers for its grey-green silky foliage. In the garden it is useful as ground cover. 20♦

Right: **Agapanthus 'Headbourne Hybrids'**
These beautiful plants are hardy, except in the coldest and wettest areas. Their handsome flowers, in varying shades of blue, are borne on stout stems up to 90cm (3ft) high. 19♦

Above: **Anaphalis yedoensis**
*The papery white 'everlasting'
flowers are carried on stems 60cm*
*(24in) tall above broad green leaves
that are white felted beneath. Soak
the stems before drying in winter.* 21♦

Acanthus mollis
(Bear's breeches)
- **Sunny position**
- **Well-drained soil**
- **Late summer flowering**

This attractive architectural plant has green glossy foliage; the mauve-pink foxglove-like flowers are rather sparingly produced on stems 120cm (4ft) or higher. As plants can spread as much as 90cm (3ft), in small gardens it is advisable not to grow more than one plant; its roots can be invasive. Any good fertile soil suits acanthus, provided it is well drained. Plant in spring, and during the first winter, especially in cold districts, give a mulch of leaf-mould or well-rotted garden compost.

A. spinosus is similar in many respects, except that it has nasty spines at the end of each dark green, deeply divided leaf. Each leaf is about 60-90cm (2-3ft) long. The flowers of *A. spinosus* are borne more freely; when dried they have a pleasant scent. The dried flowers are used for winter decorations.

Propagate by seed sown in spring in a cold frame; or by root cuttings in late autumn or winter; or by division in spring.

Take care
Protect from frost and drying winds in their first winter. 12♦

Achillea filipendulina
(Fern-leaf yarrow)
- **Sunny position**
- **Tolerates dry soils**
- **Summer flowering**

The large yellow plate-like flowers of *A. filipendulina* are best seen in the variety 'Gold Plate'; this most spectacular plant has flat bright-yellow heads at the top of stout erect stems 150cm (5ft) tall. Each flowerhead can be as much as 13cm (5in) across, and the plant can spread as much as 45cm (18in).

A more recent introduction is called 'Coronation Gold'; this has pale yellow flat heads, and the 90cm (3ft) stems rise out of grey-green feathery foliage.

Propagate by seeds or division in spring, or by cuttings in early summer. Plant in spring, in good retentive soil. A few peasticks will be needed to protect the heavy heads in wet weather, particularly in windswept gardens.

The tall varieties should be cut down to ground level during the autumn. The flowerheads can be dried for winter decoration indoors.

Take care
Plant this species in a sheltered spot, if possible. 13♦

 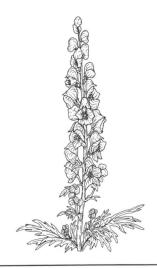

Achillea millefolium 'Cerise Queen'

(Yarrow; Milfoil)
- **Sunny position**
- **Well-drained soil**
- **Summer flowering**

Although the common yarrow *A. millefolium* can become a headache to the lawn purist, the variety 'Cerise Queen' is quite attractive. It has wide flattish heads of rose-cerise flowers, each floret with a paler centre, on stout 60cm (24in) stems in summer. The dark green feathery foliage makes a mat-like plant. It is ideal for the front of the border, but beware – it can become invasive.

Propagate either by sowing seed in spring in a cold house or frame, or by taking cuttings in early summer, again in a cold house or frame, or by division in autumn. A few stout peasticks inserted around the plants will prevent them being blown over in windy gardens.

The varieties of *Achillea* will grace any border with summer colour. For best results plant them in well-drained soil in a sunny position.

Take care
Plant this species in a sheltered spot, if possible. 13♦

Aconitum napellus

(Monkshood; Wolf's bane; Helmet flower)
- **Full sun; tolerates partial shade**
- **Fertile, retentive soil**
- **Summer and late summer flowering**

Possibly this plant is sometimes known as wolf's bane because its roots are poisonous, but this need not stop us having these stately delphinium-like flowering plants in our gardens. The blue helmet-shaped flowers are held at the top of stout 90-120cm (3-4ft) stems, and clothed with dark green finger-like foliage. To-day there are many varieties to choose from, and among the finest are 'Blue Sceptre', with blue and white bicolour flowers, 60cm (24in) stems, and a pretty neat dwarf plant; 'Bressingham Spire', a taller grower, with 90cm (3ft) stems; and the common monkshood, *A. napellus*, with indigo-blue flowers in late summer. *A. wilsonii* is also worth trying, with flowering stems up to 180cm (6ft) in late summer.

Propagate by seeds in spring or by division in spring or autumn. Plant out in late autumn.

Take care
A spring mulch of compost, and thinning out of surplus stems, will both improve flowering. 14♦

Actaea alba
(Baneberry)
- **Partial shade**
- **Moist, fertile soil**
- **Late summer and early autumn flowering**

The common name, baneberry, is due to the poisonous berries. *A. alba*, from eastern North America, has white flowers, and fresh green foliage similar to that of astilbe. The fluffy white flowers, on rather thin wiry stems up to 90cm (3ft) tall, later change to pea-sized white berries. The red baneberry, *A. rubra*, from North America has bright scarlet berries above green fern-like foliage on 45cm (18in) stems in early autumn. *A. spicata* is similar to *A. rubra* except that it has shining black berries. This is a useful plant to grow among shrubs. Be careful during the winter not to disturb the roots, as the stems and foliage die right down.

Propagate by fresh seeds in spring, but avoid using old seed; or divide the roots in spring. Choose a cool, partially shaded spot in retentive fertile soil.

Take care
Keep moist.

Agapanthus
- **Sunny position**
- **Moist, fertile soil**
- **Summer flowering**

The blue African lily, *Agapanthus umbellatus*, belongs to the family Liliaceae, but is not, in fact, a lily; it is hardy out of doors only in gardens that are usually frost-free. Today, however, there are some very fine garden forms that are hardy. During the 1950s and 1960s the 'Headbourne Hybrids' were developed from *A. campanulatus*; they are in varying shades of blue.

All agapanthus plants have lily-like flowers that are arranged in an umbel, ie like an upturned umbrella. The flowers are borne on stoutish stems, 60-90cm (2-3ft) high. They are deciduous, and the dark green strap-like foliage dies down in the winter, so it is wise to mark the spot where they grow so that when the border is dug over, the plants are not damaged. Choose moist rather than dry soil, but avoid very wet ground.

Propagate by division in spring, as the new growth appears.

Take care
Avoid deep planting. 15♦

Alchemilla mollis

(Lady's mantle)
● **Not fussy where it grows**
● **Avoid very wet ground**
● **Early summer flowering**

Since the Second World War and the great rise of interest in flower arranging, *A. mollis* has become very popular for this purpose. The rounded silky-haired pale grey-green leaves and tiny sulphur-yellow frothy sprays of flowers last a long while, beautifying either the flower border or the flower arranger's vase. This precious plant is also a superb ground cover plant. Its seeds can be invasive, however; to prevent it spreading, remove the flowerheads before the seeds ripen, and this will save many self-sown seedlings appearing where they are not wanted. It grows to about 45cm (18in) in height. *A. mollis* has the useful ability of being able to grow happily beneath trees or in full shade.

Propagate by division in spring or autumn. Plant this species in any good fertile soil, in sun or shade. Insert twiggy sticks for support in windswept locations.

Take care
Put this plant where it can spread. 14♦

Alstroemeria aurantiaca

(Peruvian lily)
● **Sun or partial shade**
● **Deep, well-drained sandy soil**
● **Summer flowering**

This is the easiest of the alstroemerias and hardier than most species. Lax leafy stems carry umbels of a dozen or more orange lily-like flowers, each up to 4cm (1.6in) long; the stems are 90cm (3ft) high. They have fleshy finger-like roots, which can be invasive once established; for this reason, put them in a bed or border where they can romp away on their own. The flowers are loved by floral arrangers because they are long lasting.

When planting, lay out the roots in the ground 15-20cm (6-8in) deep. Plant between early autumn and early spring. If the soil is heavy, especially clay soils, work in a mixture of moistened peat and sand at the base of each planting hole. Do not be surprised if there is poor or no growth the first year after planting, but once established there will be no stopping this alstroemeria. Propagate by division or by seed.

Take care
The soil should contain humus.

Alstroemeria ligtu
(Ligtu hybrids)
- **Sunny position**
- **Well-drained deep sandy soil**
- **Early summer flowering**

The ligtu hybrids are not as hardy or as easy to establish as *A. aurantiaca*. If, however, they can be grown against a sunny and sheltered wall, once established one's patience will be well rewarded. The trumpet-shaped lily-like flowers vary from yellow to flame orange, deep pink, or pale rose; they are superb as cut flowers as they are long lasting in water. The stems are up to 120cm (4ft) tall. Ligtu hybrids must have shelter and well-drained light sandy soil. Plant the tubers no less than 15cm (6in) deep in late summer or early autumn, or pot-grown seedlings in spring. When purchasing these hybrids try to buy yearling dormant tubers.

Propagate by seed, but the seedlings are hard to rear and resent being moved. Sow seeds as soon as ripe in a mixture of soil, peat, leaf-mould and sharp sand, covering the seed 1cm (0.4in) deep.

Take care
Protect young growth against frosts until tubers are fully established.

Anaphalis yedoensis
(Pearly everlasting)
- **Sun or partial shade**
- **Well-drained soil**
- **Late summer or autumn flowering**

This plant has broad green leaves that are white felted beneath, and flat papery white flowerheads with enchanting yellow centres. These develop from late summer through to early autumn, reaching up to 10cm (4in) across each flowerhead. Although its foliage dies back in the winter, silvery-white shoots soon appear as spring approaches. It will reach a height of 60cm (24in). When pearly everlasting flowers are gathered for drying, for use in winter flower arrangements, give the stems a good drink before hanging them up to dry off. *A. yedoensis* is best when grown in full sun, although it can tolerate the shade of a wall (but not of trees).

Propagate by division in autumn, or by seeds sown out of doors in spring. Plant them in any good retentive soil.

Take care
These plants will soon droop if they get too dry at the root, so keep them moist. 16♦

Anchusa azurea
(Alkanet; Italian bugloss)
- **Sunny position**
- **Well-drained soil**
- **Early summer flowering**

The anchusas are tall coarse-growing branching herbaceous perennials that have rough hairy stems and foliage with charming large forget-me-not blue flowers. *A. azurea* is still sometimes also known as *A. italica*. There are several excellent varieties: 'Morning Glory' is bright blue, and reaches 150-180cm (5-6ft); 'Opal' is an old favourite, soft blue, 150cm (5ft); 'Royal Blue', rich royal blue, 90cm (3ft); and the late spring to early summer flowering 'Loddon Royalist', gentian blue, 90cm (3ft). Anchusas will grow in any good soil. Choose young plants when setting them out in a border.

Propagation is easy. Cut roots into lengths of about 4cm (1.6in), making a clean cut at the top of each and a slanting one at the base – this will prevent them being inserted upside down. Place pots of these roots in an unheated frame. Plant out in early mid-spring.

Take care
Stake early to prevent damage. 33♦

Anemone × hybrida
(Windflower)
- **Sun or partial shade**
- **Good ordinary soil**
- **Early autumn flowering**

Of all the many windflowers, the best-known are the many hybrids of the Japanese anemones *A. × hybrida* (also known as *A. japonica*). These vary in height from 45 to 120cm (18-48in), and their individual flowers vary in size from 4 to 6cm (1.6-2.4in) across, each with five or more petals. Each flower has a central boss of yellow stamens. The stems are clothed with vine-like leaves. Their roots are like stiff black leather bootlaces. Choose from the following selection: 'Bressingham Glow', a semi-double rosy red, 45cm (18in) tall; 'Luise Uhink', white, 90cm (3ft); 'September Charm', single soft pink, 45cm (18in); 'White Queen', 90-120cm (3-4ft); and 'Honorine Jobert', white, 120cm (4ft).

Propagate by cutting the roots into 4-5cm (1.6-2in) lengths and inserting them in a deep box filled with peat and sand mixture.

Take care
Good drainage is needed, and preferably a sunny position. 34♦

Anthemis tinctoria

(Yellow-flowered chamomile; Ox-eye chamomile; Golden Marguerite)
● **Full sun**
● **Well-drained soil**
● **Summer flowering**

This species is a free-flowering herbaceous perennial. The daisy flowers are held on single-flowered stems above a base of parsley-like foliage.

There are several named varieties, varying in height from 60 to 90cm (2-3ft). The pale primrose-yellow 'E.C. Buxton' is 60-75cm (24-30in) tall; 'Loddon' has deep buttercup-yellow flowers, 75-90cm (30-36in) high; of similar height is the bright golden-yellow 'Grallagh Gold', which has flowers almost 6.5cm (2.6in) across; and the 60-90cm (2-3ft) 'Wargrave' has lemon-yellow flowers.

Propagate this species by division in spring. To encourage good strong basal growth before winter, cut the plants down as soon as they have finished flowering.

Take care
Cut plants down immediately after they have flowered. 34♦

Aquilegia hybrids

(Columbine)
● **Sun or partial shade**
● **Any well-drained fertile soil**
● **Early summer flowering**

The many hybrid strains of aquilegia are elegant plants. The 'long-spurred hybrids' have rather glaucous foliage. The flowers range in colour from pure white, through yellow to pink, soft rose, red, crimson, purple, and blue. Good effects can be had by growing these 90cm (3ft) tall plants in partial shade in the dappled light given by deciduous trees. Provided they are grown in well-drained fertile soil that does not dry out, they will give a good account of themselves.

The common columbine *Aquilegia vulgaris* and its double form are short-spurred and these, too, come in a variety of colours. They reach 60cm (24in) in height.

Propagate by seeds sown in a cool greenhouse or frame in spring, or out of doors in early summer. Division of named varieties can take place in early spring.

Take care
In full sun the flowers drop quickly; dappled sunlight gives a longer season of bloom. 35♦

Armeria plantaginea 'Bee's Ruby'
(Thrift; Sea pink)
- **Sunny position**
- **Well-drained soil**
- **Early summer flowering**

This large-flowered thrift is very free-flowering. The bright rose-pink globular flowerheads are held on stout erect smooth 35-45cm (14-18in) stalks, above dense cushion-like hummocks. The round flowerheads have papery petals. The long broad leaves, 8mm (0.3in) wide, frequently have curled edges. This popular hardy herbaceous perennial is superb as an edging. It is both a good garden plant and an excellent cut flower, as it is very long lasting.

Armerias like plenty of sun and a well-drained soil, and they are especially useful on lime or chalk soils. They are an ideal plant to grow if your garden is near the sea. Propagate them by pulling off cuttings in late summer or early autumn. You could try division but it is not easy; this also is best done in autumn.

Take care
Do not let these become waterlogged in winter.

Artemisia lactiflora
(White mugwort)
- **Sun or partial shade**
- **Moist fertile soil**
- **Late summer flowering**

This tall sturdy ornamental herbaceous perennial makes a fine clump and even in winter it has a tuft of green parsley-like foliage. Arranged at the top of its stout 150-180cm (5-6ft) stems, clothed in deeply cut chrysanthemum-like foliage, are plumes of branching sprays of milky-white scented flowers in late summer. It is good as a cut flower.

This species resents poor dry soil; it needs a good fertile soil and moisture, or the leaves and flowers will look dry and untidy. It will thrive in a sunny position given moisture at the roots and will also tolerate partial shade.

When a clump becomes worn out, lift it and replant the healthy pieces on the outside of the clump in well-prepared ground. Propagate by division in spring.

Take care
These plants must not lack moisture, if they are to give of their best.

Arum italicum 'Pictum'

(Italian arum)
- **Sun or partial shade**
- **Retentive fertile soil**
- **Spring flowering**

A. italicum has been known since 1683, but even after 300 years it is still not seen as often as it should be. However, in recent years, *A. italicum* 'Pictum' has been sought after by flower arrangers for indoor decoration. Only recently in the winter sunshine I saw an impressive clump of this particular variety, looking charming with its prettily spotted marbled foliage of grey and cream. During early summer the foliage dies down entirely, reappearing in the autumn. Greenish white spathes appear before the leaves come in spring, followed in autumn by orange-red poisonous berries. 'Pictum' is shy at flowering, not nearly as free as lords and ladies, *A. maculatum*; but its foliage is so beautiful that it is worth a place in any garden.
   It enjoys moisture, and will thrive in sunshine or partial shade. Propagate this species by taking offsets of the tubers in autumn.

Take care
Plant the tubers 10cm (4in) deep.

Aruncus sylvester

(A. dioicus)
(Goat's beard)
- **Sunshine or shade**
- **Deep rich fertile soil**
- **Summer flowering**

Goat's beard has had its botanical name changed several times, but nurserymen still use the name *A. sylvester*. It is a tall and rather handsome plant, with broad fern-like foliage on stiff wiry stems 120-150cm (4-5ft) tall; above are impressive plumes of creamy white stars throughout the summer.
   Plants make bold hummocks, which need a great deal of strength to lift out of the ground once they are well established, and even more strength when division is necessary. They do better in a deep rich fertile soil with some shade.
   The male and female flowers are on different plants; the male flowers are more feathery than the female ones, and they are not so troublesome by germinating self-sown seedlings. Even so, the female seedheads come into their own for drying. Propagate by spring-sown seed or divide clumps in late autumn.

Take care
Male plants are more free-flowering than female plants. 36◗

Asphodeline lutea

(Asphodel; King's spear)
- **Sunny position**
- **Deep sandy loam**
- **Late spring flowering**

For many years this species has also been known as *Asphodelus luteus.* It even has a third common name, Jacob's rod, which perhaps refers to its flower spikes. It is a stately looking hardy perennial. At its base there is a tuft of glabrous, dark green grassy furrowed leaves with glaucous or paler green lines. Its 90cm (3ft) erect flower spikes also carry leaves. The bright yellow fragrant silky starry-looking flowers, 1cm (0.4in) across, are arranged in buff-coloured clusters, and they will last for many weeks.

These fleshy-rooted plants are best in deep sandy loam, though I have seen plants flourishing in heavier soils. Propagate them by dividing the roots in spring or in early autumn. Take great care not to cut or damage the fleshy thong-like roots themselves.

Take care
Leave the flower spikes once they are over, as the seedheads are also decorative for the flower arranger.

Aster amellus

(Italian starwort)
- **Sunny position**
- **Retentive well-drained soil**
- **Late summer and early autumn flowering**

A. amellus has large solitary flowers with golden-yellow centres, with several clusters to each strong branching stem. The grey-green foliage is rough when handled, also the stems. These plants form a woody rootstock.

Four varieties to choose from are: 'King George', with soft blue-violet 8cm (3.2in) flowers with golden-yellow centres, introduced seventy years ago; the 60cm (24in) tall 'Nocturne', with lavender-lilac flowers; the large-flowered pink 'Sonia', 60cm (24in); and the compact dwarf 45cm (18in) 'Violet Queen'.

They object to winter wetness and are happiest in a good well-drained retentive soil. They are best planted in spring. Propagate by basal cuttings in spring, or by division where possible.

Take care
Do not let them have wet rootstocks in winter. 36-7▶

Aster × frikartii 'Mönch'

- **Sunny position**
- **Good well-drained soil**
- **Summer to autumn flowering**

Aster novae-angliae

(New England aster)
- **Sunny position**
- **Good fertile soil**
- **Late summer, early autumn flowering**

Aster × frikartii 'Mönch' is a hybrid between *A. amellus × A. thomsonii*. Its flowering period is considerably longer than *A. amellus* varieties. 'Mönch' has stout branching stems up to 90cm (3ft) bearing an abundance of clear lavender-blue flowers with yellow rayed centres, lasting until the frosts begin in autumn. Every collection of hardy herbaceous perennials should possess a plant or two.

Grow this hybrid aster in good well-drained soil in an open sunny position. Make sure that there is sufficient moisture in the soil to sustain the autumn flowers but avoid excessive wetness during the winter months.

Propagate this variety by basal cuttings in spring, or by division where possible. It is best planted in spring.

The New England aster does not seed itself about nor run its roots underground, but makes a tough vigorous compact rootstock. The leaves are rough to the touch, and a light shade of green. Beautiful clusters of flowers, each measuring up to 5cm (2in) across, are produced during the late summer and early autumn. Several lovely varieties are available, all excellent as cut flowers.

The warm pink flowers of 120cm (4ft) tall 'Harrington's Pink' were introduced 40 years ago; the semi-double phlox-purple 'Lye End Beauty' is 135cm (4.5ft) tall. Two lovely varieties are both 105cm (3.5ft) tall, 'Alma Potschke' with branching heads of salmon-tinged bright rose flowers, and the startling ruby-red 'September Ruby'.

Propagate these plants by dividing their tough rootstocks in autumn, by placing two strong forks back to back.

Take care
This plant must not have a wet rootstock in winter. 38◆

Take care
Do not let these vigorous plants exhaust the nutrients in the soil.

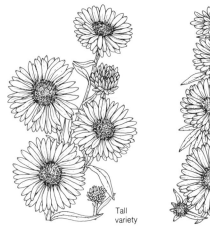
Tall variety

Dwarf variety

Aster novi-belgii

(Michaelmas daisy)
- **Sunny location**
- **Ordinary fertile soil**
- **Early autumn flowering**

The true Michaelmas daisy needs to be grown in well-enriched soil, or plants will soon exhaust the ground. Some varieties are very invasive.

Here are seven varieties to choose from: the stately purple 'Orlando' is 150cm (5ft) tall; the pure white semi-double 'Blandie' is 105-120cm (3.5-4ft) tall; the fine dark blue 'Mistress Quickly' reaches 120cm (4ft); the fully double 'Coombe Rosemary' has violet-purple flowers 3-5cm (1.25-2in) across; and 'Winston S. Churchill' has rich ruby-crimson flowers 75cm (30in) tall. A fine double is the light blue 'Marie Ballard', 90cm (36in) tall; the semi-double rich red 'Freda Ballard' has 90cm (36in) stiff straight stems. There is a good selection of dwarf hybrid *novi-belgii* Michaelmas daisies, which are free-flowering and long-lasting in bloom. 'Audrey' has large pale blue flowers, 30-40cm (12-16in) tall; of similar height is 'Blue Bouquet', a bright blue; 'Lady in Blue' has semi-double rich blue flowers, very free blooming, makes perfect little hummocks and is only 25cm (10in) high. Of the pink and red shades there is 'Little Pink Beauty', a superb semi-double 40cm (16in) tall, or the double pink 'Chatterbox', 45cm (18in); 'Dandy' is 30cm (12in), with purple-red flowers, and 'Little Red Boy', of similar height, is a deep rosy red. Finally, the late-flowering 30cm (12in) 'Snowsprite' makes perfect little hummocks.

Propagate all these by division in spring. To keep them thriving, divide and replant every three years; when doing so choose the strongest and healthiest young pieces on the outside of the clump, and resist replanting any woody pieces.

Take care
If mildew attacks, spray with flowers of sulphur. 38♦

Astilbe × arendsii
(False goat's beard)
- **Sunshine or partial shade**
- **Moist fertile soil**
- **Summer flowering**

Astilbes are one of our most
decorative hardy herbaceous
perennials. The arendsii hybrids vary
from white, through pale pink, deep
pink, coral and red, to magenta. Not
only are they good garden plants but
they also force well under glass in an
unheated greenhouse. The foliage
varies from light to dark green, with
some of purplish and reddish purple
shades. The fluffy panicles of flowers
are held on erect stems 60-90cm
(2-3ft) tall, but the dwarf varieties are
only 45cm (18in).

They will grow in full sun or partial
shade and thrive in most soils. They
have a long flowering period and
their rigid erect stems do not require
staking. There are too many varieties
to mention, but all are worth a place
in any garden.

Propagate by division in spring.
Alternatively, roots may be divided in
autumn and potted for forcing or
spring planting.

Take care
Do not cut old flower stems back
before spring. 39♦

Astrantia major
(Masterwort)
- **Sunshine or partial shade**
- **Retentive fertile soil**
- **Summer flowering**

The masterwort *A. major* is a
fascinating perennial. Each
flowerhead has outer bracts that are
stiff, papery and pointed, and in the
centre of each individual flower are
many tiny florets. The whole umbel
presents a number of star-like
flowers. The foliage is palmate. The
colour of the flowers is a pure rose-
pink, with a pinkish collar of the petal-
like bracts. The flowers are held on
wiry stems 60cm (2ft) high. Other
varieties have greenish white or pale
green collars of bracts. One variety,
'Sunningdale Variegated', has
leaves prettily splashed with yellow
and cream, but as the season
advances they lose their variegation
unless old flower stems are cut back.

To be successful, astrantias must
be in a soil that does not dry out in
summer; a thinly dappled or partial
shade is an advantage.

Propagate by seed sown as soon
as it has been gathered, or by
division in spring.

Take care
Do not let these plants become too
dry in summer. 40♦

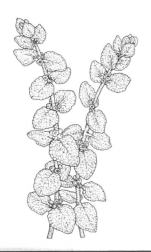

Ballota pseudodictamnus
- Sunny location
- Well-drained ordinary soil
- Summer flowering (insignificant)

This white woolly hardy perennial has a bush-like habit; it is a good ground cover and looks well throughout the year. The small mauve flowers are almost invisible, so it is the white woolly foliage that is the attraction. Established plants have a woody base, and new shoots are smothered with pale apple-green egg-shaped pointed deeply indented leaves. The many-flowered whorls of pale green bracts are widely displayed at each pair of leaves; the lower leaves remain apple-green but those nearer the top of each 45-60cm (18-24in) stem become more and more woolly. Dried ballota is much used by flower arrangers.

In late spring plants need pruning; leaves that have suffered winter damage can be cut back. Propagate by taking heel cuttings in early summer.

Take care
Give dried material a good drink before storing. 41♦

Baptisia australis
(False indigo; Blue indigo)
- Sunny location
- Good deep fertile soil
- Early summer flowering

This handsome leguminous plant is from North America, although the specific name is *australis*. Its vetch-like trifoliate leaves, on stout 75-90cm (30-36in) stems, carry 23cm (9in) branching spikes of rich blue pea-shaped lupin-like flowers in early summer. In very good fertile soil plants can reach 120cm (4ft).

For some reason, this plant is not widely grown; this may be because it takes a while before it is properly established. It is a useful hardy herbaceous perennial and can be grown from seed, but it will take two years before the plants become established. Although plants can be divided they are best left alone unless they really need transplanting. Propagate by division in autumn or early spring. Or seeds can be sown in pans or boxes and placed in a cold greenhouse in the spring.

Take care
Provide good well-enriched soil.

Bergenia cordifolia
(Pig squeak)
- **Sunshine or shade**
- **Not fussy about soil**
- **Spring flowering**

Bergenia has gone through a series of generic names: at one time it was *Megasea*, and then *Saxifraga*.

In recent years bergenias have come into their own, partly due to the interest in flower arranging. The large leathery green or dark green foliage often takes on attractive hues of red, crimson and brown-red. Their flowers, displayed on stout stems 30cm (12in) high, rise above the mass of green leathery foliage. A large clump in my garden is *B. cordifolia* 'Purpurea', which has large rounded leaves that turn to purplish hues in winter; in spring it displays bright magenta-coloured flowers.

To write about bergenias and not mention the pretty white-flowered *B. stracheyi* 'Silver Light' or 'Silberlicht' would be a bad omission. The pure white flowers take on a pinkish tint as they age, but they are still lovely.

Propagate bergenias by division, immediately after flowering or in autumn.

Take care
Do not let them dry out. 41▶

Brunnera macrophylla
(Siberian bugloss)
- **Sunshine or a little shade**
- **Damp soil**
- **Spring flowering**

B. macrophylla, when I first knew this plant, was called *Anchusa myosotidiflora,* the species name indicating that the flowers were like forget-me-nots.

It is one of the first of the border plants to produce blue flowers in spring. The basal leaves are rough, heart-shaped and large, on stalks about 38-45cm (15-18in) long, which carry sprays of small blue flowers. In the garden, young plants from self-sown seed can easily be removed and replanted to form a new clump, or given away.

There is also an attractive variegated form, *B. macrophylla* 'Variegata', which has prettily marked creamy white leaves. The variety needs a sheltered spot, and the soil must not dry out.

Propagate by root cuttings, which are like thick black leather bootlaces, or by division in early autumn.

Take care
To prevent self-sown seedlings, remove flowerheads as soon as they have faded. 42▶

Buphthalmum salicifolium

(Willow-leaf ox-eye)
- Sun or partial shade
- Good fertile soil
- Early summer to early autumn flowering

This hardy herbaceous perennial has narrow willow-like sharp-pointed leaves, slightly hairy, which clothe the stiff slender stems. The stems are crowned by masses of solitary 4cm (1.6in) wide bright golden-yellow daisy-like flowers; the narrow pointed petals are like golden stars.

It is a plant that will grow almost anywhere, and it blooms from early summer through to early autumn. If not staked, the plants will create neat tumbling bushes, 45-60cm (18-24in) high; they are better left to grow naturally. This is an ideal plant to grow near the front of the border.

Propagate *B. salicifolium* by division of the roots during spring or in the autumn. Cuttings can be taken, ideally in the summer for the best plants. Seeds sown in spring also produce good plants.

Take care
Allow them to grow informally; they do not look so attractive if staked.

Campanula lactiflora

(Milky bellflower)
- Full sun
- Deep fertile soil
- Early to late summer flowering

This is a superb perennial which will reach a height of 120-150cm (4-5ft), and in partial shade may reach 180cm (6ft), though it is better in full sun. Its stout stems require staking in windy gardens. The rootstock, although vigorous, fortunately does not rampage in the soil. The rigid stems carry loose or dense panicles of white or pale blue to deep lilac flowers. The stems are clothed with small light green leaves. The flesh-pink 'Loddon Anna' is a lovely form of *C. lactiflora*, reaching 120-150cm (4-5ft). The baby of this species, 'Pouffe', only 25cm (10in) high, is an ideal dwarf plant, with light green foliage forming mounds that are smothered for weeks with lavender-blue flowers during the early and midsummer months.

Propagate by division or by cuttings in spring

Take care
These campanulas need moisture during the growing season. 42♦

Above: **Anchusa azurea**
Lovely blue flowers adorn this plant in midsummer. Several varieties are available, differing in height from 90 to 180cm (3-6ft). Grow in full sun, and stake plants early on. 22♦

Above:
Anemone 'Honorine Jobert'
*This lovely white form was a 'sport'
from a red-flowered variety in the
garden of M. Jobert, in 1858.* 22♦

Left: **Anthemis tinctoria
'Wargrave'**
*A fine variety with lemon yellow
flowers on 90cm (3ft) stems.* 23♦

Above right:
Aquilegia 'McKana Hybrids'
*These large-flowered hybrids have a
fine selection of beautiful colours.* 23♦

Right:
Aquilegia 'Long-spurred Hybrids'
*Elegant wiry stemmed plants that will
grow best in dappled shade.* 23♦

Above:
Aster amellus 'King George'
*This large-flowered aster has held its
popularity since it was bred in 1914.
The soft blue-violet blooms are
borne on 60cm (2ft) stems.* 26♦

Left: **Aruncus sylvester**
*This handsome and tenacious hardy
herbaceous perennial has
magnificent plumes of creamy white
flowers in the summer. Grow it in
some shade in deep fertile soil.* 25♦

Right: **Aster amellus 'Nocturne'**
*This recommended variety has a
compact bushy habit and semi-
double lilac-lavender flowers in
summer. Grow it in free-draining soil
and avoid winter wetness.* 26♦

Above: **Aster × frikartii 'Mönch'**
*A splendid hybrid that blooms earlier
and for a longer period than the* Aster
amellus *varieties. Its 75cm (30in)
stems carry lavender-blue flowers
well into the autumn.* 27♦

Below: **Aster novi-belgii 'Orlando'**
*Panicles of pink-purple 5cm (2in)
flowers are freely borne on stems up
to 150cm (5ft) in height during the
autumn. These plants need a fertile
soil and a sunny location.* 28♦

Above: **Astilbe × arendsii**
These hardy herbaceous perennials are ideal in a garden where the soil does not dry out. Astilbes flower over a long period and do not need to be staked. Good for sun or shade. 29\blacktriangleright

Above: **Astrantia major**
For those who favour 'everlasting flowers' the paper-like florets of the astrantias are very attractive. Dappled shade and a moist soil suit these summer-flowering plants. 29\blacktriangleright

Above: **Ballota pseudodictamnus**
This compact plant is grown for its white woolly foliage rather than for the insignificant purple blooms. Excellent for drying for indoor decoration during the winter. 30♦

Below: **Bergenia cordifolia**
Clusters of attractive pink-purple flowers are produced in spring on robust stems. Towards autumn the fleshy leaves take on a bronze colour that gives added interest. 31♦

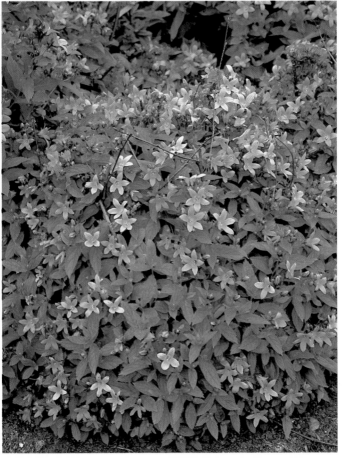

Left: **Brunnera macrophylla**
Tiny blue flowers appear above the large hairy leaves of this plant during the spring months. 31♦

Below left:
Campanula lactiflora 'Pouffe'
This charming miniature campanula has little green hummocks covered in lavender-blue flowers. 32♦

Right: **Centaurea macrocephala**
Striking golden flowerheads borne on erect stems up to 120cm (4ft) in height make this plant a handsome addition to the summer garden. 50♦

Below: **Chelone obliqua**
A perennial with unusually shaped flowers that resemble a turtle's head. Do not grow near weaker plants; it will spread quickly. 52♦

Left: **Chrysanthemum maximum**
*Every garden should contain a clump
of these dependable perennials.
They tolerate all soils and are
available with single or double
blooms. Excellent as cut flowers.* 52♦

Right: **Convallaria majalis**
*Admired by all, the fresh green
foliage and pure white fragrant
flowers are a delight in spring. This
lovely plant will thrive in light shade
and moist conditions.* 54♦

Below: **Cimicifuga japonica**
*At 90cm (3ft) tall, this is the smallest
of the cimicifugas. The elegant
racemes of snow white blooms
appear in midsummer. Grow in moist
fertile soil for best results.* 53♦

Above: **Coreopsis verticillata**
The starry yellow flowers borne from midsummer to autumn on stiff stems are ideal for flower arranging. Be sure to keep the plant well watered during hot dry weather. 55♦

Right: **Cortaderia selloana 'Sunningdale Silver'**
This splendid variety of pampas grass produces creamy white plumes about 210cm (7ft) high during the autumn. Keep moist in hot dry weather. 55♦

Below: **Corydalis lutea**
This adaptable perennial keeps on flowering throughout the summer. Plants will seed freely, but self-sown seedlings can be cleared easily. 56♦

Above: **Dicentra spectabilis**
Planted in a position sheltered from wind and frost, this charming plant will bloom in early summer. 59♦

Below: **Dictamnus albus**
Spikes of fragrant white flowers appear in early summer above the finely divided foliage. 59♦

Campanula persicifolia
(Peach-leaved bellflower)
- **Sun or partial shade**
- **Good fertile soil**
- **Summer flowering**

The peach-leaved bellflower is a perennial with an evergreen basal rosette of pleasing dark green foliage. It reaches a height of about 60cm (24in), but named varieties will be about 90cm (36in) tall. The slender stems carry numerous open cup-shaped bell-like flowers.

Varieties include: the large double white 'Fleur de Neige', with cup-shaped flowers, 7cm (2.75in) wide, on stiff stems 75-90cm (30-36in) tall; the semi-double 'Pride of Exmouth', with rich lavender-blue flowers on 60cm (24in) slender stems; and the new variety 'Hampstead White', with single cup-and-saucer flowers on 70cm (28in) stems.

Propagate by division in spring, or take basal cuttings in early autumn. As this campanula is surface rooting, its life expectancy is not as long as some perennials; lift, divide and replant it in spring every third year. Rust can disfigure the foliage; pick off affected leaves and spray plant.

Take care
Replant stock every third year.

Catananche caerulae
(Cupid's dart)
- **Full sun**
- **Well-drained light soil**
- **Summer flowering**

This attractive cornflower-like perennial forms clumps of hairy grass-like leaves, from which emerge 60cm (24in) spikes each carrying silvery papery bracts and lavender-blue everlasting flowers. The best form, *C. caerulea* 'Major', has larger and richer blue flowers. There is also a white variety, 'Perry's White'.

To extend the season of flowering, grow two or more clumps, and cut one down when it comes into flower; this will then bloom later. The flowers can be cut and dried, like everlastings, and used for indoor decoration. All catananches are best in full sun and in well-drained soil. If plants are cut back in early autumn, this enables them to pull through the winter.

Propagate by root cuttings in autumn, or by division in spring, or by seeds sown out of doors in spring.

Take care
These plants should have good drainage.

Centaurea macrocephala

(Yellow hardhead; Yellow hardweed)
- Full sun
- Light, sandy soil
- Summer flowering

This member of the knapweed family is a very handsome perennial, the strong erect stems of which are 90-120cm (3-4ft) tall; at the top of each stem appears a round golden flowerhead, as large as a tennis ball. Each flower is surrounded by rough brown papery bracts forming a collar that protects the inner florets. If situated in the middle of a border this plant makes an outstanding individual display. The flowerheads dry well, and are useful for winter decorations for the flower arranger.

It would be wrong not to mention *C. dealbata* 'John Coutts'; this perennial cornflower is free-flowering and, from my experience, can be left in one position for many years. The cornflower blooms are large and clear pink, on 90cm (3ft) stems.

Propagate when necessary by division in spring or autumn.

Take care
These plants need full sun, and will do well in a limy soil. 43♦

Centranthus ruber

(Red valerian)
- Full sun
- Ordinary garden soil
- Summer flowering

Although this perennial may be classed as a wilding, it is worth garden space, especially if you have a lime or chalk soil, as this is something it revels in. Plants can often be seen growing on old walls or mortar rubble dumps. The closely packed heads of red or deep pink flowers are carried on 60-90cm (2-3ft) glaucous stems and foliage. The red flowers are certainly more colourful than the pink ones, and it is as well to remember this when buying. There is also a white form available, *Centranthus ruber* 'Albus'.

Propagate by seeds sown out of doors during late spring or the seeds can be sown as soon as they are ripe where the plants will eventually flower. Alternatively, plants can be divided in late autumn or spring.

This plant has also been known as *Kentranthus ruber*.

Take care
Choose a well-coloured form when buying.

Cephalaria gigantea

(Giant scabious)
- **Sunny location**
- **Any good ordinary soil**
- **Early summer flowering**

What fun botanists have in changing names. For years I have known this giant scabious-like plant as *C. tartarica*, which indicates that it comes from Central Asia. Nevertheless, *C. gigantea* is a good name for this spectacular hardy herbaceous perennial, as it grows up to 180cm (6ft); it needs to be planted near the back of a border, or, if you have island beds, then place these plants in the centre. It has large, deeply toothed leaves, soft green above and paler beneath. The large heads of light yellow flowers grow on 60cm (2ft) branching stalks. The flowers last for several weeks during the early summer.

Propagate this plant by dividing the stout roots in spring or by sowing seeds out of doors in spring and transplanting the seedlings in late spring.

Take care
Do not put this tall handsome cephalaria in front of shorter plants.

Ceratostigma willmottianum

(Hardy plumbago)
- **Full sun**
- **Fertile well-drained soil**
- **Late summer and autumn flowering**

This plant is generally found in nurserymen's shrub catalogues, but its treatment is almost identical with that of fuchsias; it has to be cut back in late winter or very early spring to encourage strong new growth for the coming season. It makes a wiry, bushy plant up to 90cm (3ft) tall; its small rough leaves are green, set on brown twiggy stems that are topped by branching shoots bearing clear cobalt-blue flowers.

Two plants that I was told were *C. willmottianum* were in fact *C. plumbaginoides*. The stems are 30cm (12in) high, and in late autumn dark blue bristly flowers are borne at the end of each stem. This is an ideal plant for the front of a border.

Propagate *C. willmottianum* by softwood cuttings in early summer, inserted in a heated propagator. Take half-ripe cuttings from *C. plumbaginoides* in midsummer, or divide in spring.

Take care
Grow these in well-drained soil.

Chelone obliqua
(Turtlehead)
- Sun; tolerates light shade
- Fertile well-drained soil
- Autumn flowering

This rather strange-looking
perennial derives its popular name
from the unusual shape of the
flowers. It is a close relation of the
penstemons and is sometimes
confused with them. Its dark green
leaves are broad to oblong in shape,
5-20cm (2-8in) long, and arranged in
pairs, the last two being just below
the erect crowded truss of rosy-
purple flowers. The square stems
are 60-90cm (2-3ft) tall. Provided it is
given a sunny position in the border,
this plant will produce blooms for
several weeks in autumn: the
flowers are very weather resistant,
which is useful in wet seasons. Its
roots have a spreading habit, and
plants soon form a mat.

Propagate by seed sown in spring
under glass in a temperature of 13-
18°C (55-65°F), or in late spring
without heat in a cold frame; or by
division of roots in spring, or in late
autumn as soon as the flowers fade.

Take care
Chelones may crowd out less tough
growing plants. 43♦

Chrysanthemum maximum
(Shasta daisy)
- Sunny location
- Any good fertile soil
- Summer flowering

The Shasta daisy, a native of the
Pyrenees, is a must for any perennial
border. The height varies from 60 to
90cm (2-3ft). The flowers are single
or double, with plain or fringed
petals. On account of the large flat
heads, rain and wind can soon knock
plants over; short peasticks should
be inserted in the ground before the
plants are too advanced.

One of the best-known varieties is
'Esther Read', 45cm (18in) tall, with
pure white, fully double flowers;
'Wirral Pride' is a 90cm (36in) beauty
with large anemone-centred
blooms; another variety is the fully
double white-flowered 'Wirral
Supreme', 80cm (32in) high. If you
prefer a large, fully double frilly-
flowered variety, plant 'Droitwich
Beauty', 80-90cm (32-36in) tall; a
creamy-yellow variety is 'Mary
Stoker', 80cm (32in) high.

Propagate by softwood cuttings in
summer, or by division in autumn or
spring.

Take care
Be sure to provide support. 44♦

Cimicifuga racemosa
(Black snake-root; Bugbane)
- **Sun or partial shade**
- **Rich fertile moist soil**
- **Summer flowering**

This plant is commonly known as bugbane because of the rather unpleasant smell that is given off by the leaves of some species. Such a name is misleading, however, as no perennial can be more beautiful when its tall branching stems are displaying the feathery sprays of creamy-white flowers during late summer. The stems are 150-180cm (5-6ft) tall. The fluffy flowers droop gracefully above shining green divided foliage. Another fine cimicifuga is *C. japonica,* with snow white blooms on stems up to 90cm (3ft) tall.

Cimicifugas will grow in dry soils but are far finer where their roots are growing in rich deep well-cultivated soil, preferably moist. Propagate them by seed sown as soon as it has been gathered, or by division in spring or autumn.

Take care
This plant needs full sun, and must not become dry or starved. 44-5♦

Clematis heracleifolia
(Tube clematis)
- **Sunny location**
- **Ordinary fertile soil**
- **Late summer flowering**

This species is popularly called the tube clematis because of its tube-shaped flowers. It is not a climbing plant, but a hardy herbaceous perennial, bearing clusters of sweetly scented flowers resembling the individual florets of a hyacinth. Clusters of small purple-blue flowers are borne on leafy stems about 60-90cm (2-3ft) in height. Later, frothy seedheads provide an added bonus. The form called *C.h. davidiana* has large leaves that are slightly coarse in texture; it bears clusters of deliciously scented rich blue hyacinth-like flowers on 90-120cm (3-4ft) stems.

Propagate by division during the dormant season. Both *Clematis heracleifolia* and *C.h. davidiana* need to have all their top growth cut back and the previous season's dead shoots removed during the winter.

Take care
Remove all dead shoots and cut the plants back in spring.

Clematis recta
(Herbaceous virgin's bower)
- **Full sun**
- **Ordinary fertile soil**
- **Summer flowering**

This outstanding hardy perennial clematis has pinnate glistening dark green leaves. During the summer an abundance of billowing sweetly scented white flowers is carried on branching sprays at the top of straggling stems. Each flower forms a star and can be as much as 2.5cm (1in) across. Plants reach a height of 120-150cm (4-5ft), and sometimes higher. Place a few peasticks around the plant, allowing the stems to clamber through them; in autumn, when flowering has finished, the mound will be covered with clouds of silvery seedheads.

This fine clematis will thrive in full sun in ordinary garden soil, and also do well in an alkaline soil. A spring mulch of peat or rotted manure will be beneficial.

Propagate this species by division during the dormant season.

Take care
Prune the plant down to ground level during the winter.

Convallaria majalis
(Lily of the valley)
- **Light shade or dappled sun**
- **Retentive fertile soil**
- **Late spring flowering**

Lily of the valley is one of the best-loved sweetly scented perennials. This shade-loving plant enjoys liberal supplies of humus in the soil. On occasions it is recommended as suitable to grow under trees, but this is not so, as tree roots take moisture and nourishment from the soil; some sunshine is preferable, provided moisture and humus are available.

Plant in early autumn; the stoloniferous roots should be placed 7.5-10cm (3-4in) beneath the surface, with the fleshy crowns pointing upwards about 2.5cm (1in) under the surface. Keep the ground moist from spring to autumn. A top dressing of rotted farmyard manure, garden compost or leaf-mould should be given annually. When picking, pull the flower stems carefully, leaving a pair of leaves; if you must have leaves, pull only one from each crown. Propagate by division in early autumn.

Take care
The plants must always have plenty of moisture and humus. 45♦

Coreopsis verticillata

(Tickseed)
- **Full sun**
- **Fertile soil**
- **Summer and autumn flowering**

This plant from the eastern United States is one of the best perennials for the front of the border. It makes a dense bushy plant; the deep green foliage is finely divided, on stiff needle-like stems that support bright yellow starry flowers as much as 4cm (1.6in) across, and the blooms have a very long season. The flowers are fine for cutting, and mix particularly well with the light lavender-blue flowers of Aster × frikartii hybrids. Coreopsis must not be left in the same place too long without being lifted and divided, or the plants will become starved. This species does not require support

Today there is also an improved and larger-flowered variety called C. verticillata 'Grandiflora', which has warmer yellow flowers than the species.

Propagate this plant by division in spring.

Take care
Do not let this plant dry out in warm weather; water in the evening. 46♦

Cortaderia selloana

(Pampas grass)
- **Full sun**
- **Light retentive fertile soil**
- **Late summer and early autumn flowering**

Pampas grass has masses of gracefully arching leaves that forms a good base for the erect stems to carry their silky silvery white plumes. For indoor decoration gather plumes as soon as they are fully developed.

Varieties include: 'Monstrosa', creamy-white plumes, 275cm (9ft) stems; compact 'Pumila', with short foliage, creamy white plumes, erect 150cm (5ft) stems; 'Sunningdale Silver', creamy white open plumes, 210cm (7ft) stems; 'Rendatleri', silver-pink plumes, 180-240cm (6-8ft) stems.

They are not fussy over soil but are happiest in light soils enriched with humus or well rotted farmyard manure or good garden compost. Plant in either autumn or spring. Winter care entails allowing the grass to die down. Never cut it with shears; wear stout leather gloves to pull the leaves out of established clumps.

Propagate by seed under glass in spring, or by division in spring.

Take care
Give ample moisture during very hot weather. 10, 47♦

Corydalis lutea

(Yellow fumitory)
- **Sunny location**
- **Any well-drained soil**
- **Late spring to late summer flowering**

The yellow fumitory may be only a wilding, but its small bright yellow trumpet-like flowers, which rise among a hummock of soft divided pretty fern-like foliage, in all about 30cm (12in) tall, are well worth growing. This charming little plant will make a gay display from late spring and throughout the summer, well into the autumn. It will readily naturalize once it is established.

Although it can often be seen flourishing in old walls, it also looks well when growing in odd places where perhaps other plants could not or would not exist.

Propagate by sowing seed out of doors in spring, where they are to flower; but plants may also be divided in spring. Self-sown seedlings will appear profusely; keep them in check by uprooting any unwanted ones regularly.

Take care
Keep plants in check. 46◆

Crambe cordifolia

(Flowering seakale)
- **Full sun**
- **Good rich soil**
- **Early summer flowering**

To many people the common name of seakale will conjure up that most delectable blanched vegetable, but *Crambe cordifolia* is a dramatic perennial; some authorities say it is for only the larger garden, but there is nothing to stop the small garden having an isolated plant. This magnificent species has large deep unequally lobed and toothed heart-shaped leaves, 30-90cm (24-36in) long. From a mound of foliage arise 150-180cm (5-6ft) flower spikes on which massive branching sprays of hundreds of small white flowers appear. The width of one plant can be as much as its height.

Propagate by root cuttings taken off after flowering has ceased, or by seed sown out of doors in spring, but it will be three years before seedling plants will flower. As a perennial it is not long lasting; therefore restock with a new plant.

Take care
Spray it with malathion if the cabbage white fly attacks.

Crocosmia masonorum

(Montbretia)
- **Sun or partial shade**
- **Light sandy fertile well-drained soil**
- **Summer flowering**

Montbretia is probably known by most gardeners, but *C. masonorum* is rather special. There are two main differences: the striking ribbed strap-like foliage is broader than that of montbretia (*Crocosmia × crocosmiiflora*); and the intense flame-orange flowers of *C. masonorum* are carried on top of the arching stems, instead of being arranged beneath the stems.

When this crocosmia became popular around 1953, it was considered not to be fully hardy. Ten years later it came through the winter of 1963, when its corms were encased in 50cm (20in) of ice, so it must surely be termed hardy. The corms are small, and the first year after planting they are shy to flower, but planted 15cm (6in) apart and left alone for three or four years, they will soon create a splendid clump. Divide corms in early spring.

Take care
Do not lift and replant while the corms are doing well.

Curtonus paniculatus

(Aunt Liza)
- **Full sun**
- **Light well-drained fertile soil**
- **Late summer flowering**

The strange common name came about because this species used to be known as *Antholyza paniculata*. This South African perennial has large dark green sword-like foliage, 3-8cm (1.2-3.2in) wide, bearing many orange-red montbretia-like flowers in a zig-zag fashion on stems up to 120cm (4ft). The tuberous roots form a large flat mass just below the soil surface.

This plant does well in any light well-drained soil, in a sunny position. Before planting, work in leaf-mould and sharp sand; place the corms 5cm (2in) below soil level. Within three years a mass of corms will become visible above the soil, forming a thick clump; when this happens they should be lifted, divided and replanted in spring. Propagate by division in spring.

Take care
Choose a well-drained sunny site, as this species dislikes wet heavy soils.

Delphinium
Belladonna varieties

(Perennial larkspur)
- **Full sun**
- **Deep rich well-drained retentive soil**
- **Summer and autumn flowering**

Belladonna delphiniums are bushy, and their deeply cut foliage produces stems that display branched spikes of pretty blue flowers. The majority of belladonnas do not require staking, except in very windswept gardens. As a group they are also stronger and easier to cultivate than their taller sisters. The Belladonna delphiniums available today are the result of selection and hybridization that has been performed throughout the 20th century.

The gentian-blue 'Wendy' is 120cm (4ft) tall. Three varieties just over 90cm (3ft) tall are 'Pink Sensation' (cerise-pink), 'Moerheim' (white) and the semi-double 'Naples' (brilliant blue).

Propagate these delphiniums by division or by cuttings rooted in a cold frame, in spring.

Take care
Avoid cold wet soils, and plant in spring.

Dianthus

(Garden pinks)
- **Full sun**
- **Well-drained rich soil**
- **Early summer flowering**

Varieties of garden pinks include: 'Mrs Simkins', with scented double white flowers 20cm (8in) high; the sweetly scented semi-double pale pink 'Inchmery', 30cm (12in); the double 'White Ladies', 45cm (18in); and the double salmon-pink 30cm (12in) 'Doris'.

The main requirement of garden pinks is a well-drained open soil with plenty of humus, rotted farmyard manure, rotted garden compost and an ample supply of lime or old mortar rubble; however, they will flourish in an acid soil. To encourage new growth cut them back when the plants have finished flowering. The new growth will enable them to withstand the winter, and provide propagating material. Plant garden pinks in early autumn so that they become established before winter. Propagate them by cuttings taken from non-flowering basal shoots, or by layering in midsummer.

Take care
Suport taller varieties with twigs.

Dicentra spectabilis

(Bleeding heart; Dutchman's breeches)
- **Partial shade or full sun**
- **Rich well-cultivated fertile soil**
- **Late spring and early summer flowering**

This charming plant has a fragile look; the glaucous finely divided foliage has attractive arching sprays off the stoutish stems, about 60cm (2ft) high, sometimes taller, from which dangle crimson and white lockets. When open, the flowers are rosy pink with white tips. It makes a good cut flower, and roots potted in autumn can be forced into flower in an unheated greenhouse.

These delicate-looking plants can be damaged by late spring frosts, and it is advisable to plant them where the sun does not reach the plants before the frost has gone. Plant *D. spectabilis* where it can be protected by a wall or evergreen shrubs. A mulch of leaf-mould or well-rotted garden compost should be given each spring.

Propagate in spring by cutting the roots with a sharp knife, or by root cuttings taken in spring and rooted in an unheated frame.

Take care
Protect against wind and frost. 48♦

Dictamnus albus

(Burning bush)
- **Full sun**
- **Well-drained deep fertile soil**
- **Early summer flowering**

The burning bush so called because on hot dry days, when the seedpods are ripening, it is possible by holding a lighted match at the base of the flower stalk to ignite the volatile oil given off by the plant without doing any damage to the dictamnus itself. Other common names that have been used for this plant are dittany and fraxinella, and in America it is called gas plant.

The smooth divided light green leaves are on erect stems that are lemon scented. The erect stems bear white flowers that have very long stamens. The plant usually seen in our gardens is *D. albus purpureus,* which has soft mauve-purple flowers, veined with red. Both are 90cm (3ft) tall. As the plants are deep rooted they can remain in one place for a number of years.

Propagate by root cuttings in late autumn or winter, or by division in spring.

Take care
Give water in very dry weather. 48♦

Dierama pulcherrimum
(Wand flower)
- **Full sun**
- **Light sandy soil**
- **Late summer flowering**

The stems of this plant are clothed with grassy evergreen leaves 60cm (2ft) long. The bell-shaped purplish red to deep old rose flowers are not unlike inverted crocuses, which hang down from the graceful arching 150cm (5ft) stems. They open at the tip of the stems first, which is unusual.

This bulbous plant thrives best in a warm position, though it likes to have its root-run in the shade. Bulbs should be planted in late spring, 8-10cm (3.2-4in) deep, and should be surrounded with sharp sand. Choose well-drained porous moist soil in full sun. Once established, leave them alone until they become overcrowded.

Propagate by lifting the offsets and dividing them. It can also be raised from seed, which germinates very readily, with the seedlings surrounding the older plants.

Take care
Choose a suitably sheltered position, if growing in gardens that may be draughty or windswept.

Digitalis grandiflora
(D. ambigua)
(Yellow foxglove)
- **Sun or partial shade**
- **Ordinary soil**
- **Summer flowering**

Most gardeners are familiar with the biennial common foxglove, *D. purpurea,* but the yellow foxglove, *D. grandiflora,* is a perennial evergreen. It has normal 5cm (2in) foxglove flowers in a pale creamy yellow, prettily blotched with brown spots. The individual flowers are smaller than those of the common foxglove, but it has a larger quantity of flower spikes. The whole plant is hairy. The oblong leaves, notched at the edges, clasp the 60cm (24in) stems.

Foxgloves grow in ordinary garden soil, but the ground needs humus to prevent the plants drying out during hot weather. To guard against root rot ensure that the soil does not remain excessively wet during the winter months. Propagate by sowing seed out of doors in spring, or by division in spring.

Take care
When raising from seed, cull poor forms when seedlings bloom.

Doronicum 'Miss Mason'

(Leopard's bane)
- **Full sun or partial shade**
- **Any good fertile soil**
- **Spring flowering**

The leopard's bane is one of the first perennials to brighten the garden as spring approaches; the large yellow star-shaped flowers are a good follow-on after the early daffodils are over.

'Miss Mason' is probably a hybrid of *D. austriacum* or *D. caucasicum*. Its bright yellow daisy-like flowers are in bloom for several weeks. The smooth heart-shaped leaves have scalloped edges, and are bright green; the flowers are carried at the top of wiry stems 45cm (18in) high. This variety makes an excellent cut flower. When flowering is over, the leaves of 'Miss Mason' do not die down as this hybrid is evergreen. To have a good display, plant them in groups of five or six.

Propagate by division in early autumn or spring. Plants should be divided every third or fourth year.

Take care
Remove faded blooms so that plants produce a further crop of flowers in the autumn. 65◗

Eccremocarpus scaber

(Glory flower)
- **Full sun**
- **Any fertile soil**
- **Summer flowering**

This semi-woody perennial evergreen climber needs to be treated as an annual in cold and wet areas or where hard frosts are usual. The stems are 3.7-4.6m (12-15ft) long and at the end of each fern-like leaf is a tendril used to attach the plant to its support. The 2.5cm (1in) tubular orange-yellow and orange-scarlet flowers are carried on graceful 15-25cm (6-10in) racemes bearing 10-20 flowers.

Eccremocarpus will thrive in almost any type of soil except chalk. Grow it against a sheltered and sunny wall. Prune each spring by cutting out all dead or frosted growth, and shortening a few main shoots to produce new growth.

Propagate by seed sown under glass in a temperature of 13°C (55°F) in spring or by cuttings of ripened shoots in autumn in heat under glass.

Take care
Do not plant before late spring.

Echinacea purpurea
(Cone flower)
- **Sunny location**
- **Well-drained soil**
- **Summer flowering**

For many years this strongly-growing perennial was known as *Rudbeckia purpurea*. It is a stately plant with dark green foliage, rough to the touch, on stiff stout stems.

The rich reddish-purple flowers have a central boss of orange-brown which makes them quite outstanding. Over the years there have been many varieties raised. The variety I remember when first working in a nursery was called 'The King', 120cm (4ft) tall, and it is still available. An earlier flowering variety is the broad-petalled erect carmine-purple flowered 'Robert Bloom', which is 90cm (3ft) tall. If you want a variety of colours, the Bressingham Hybrids, also 90cm (3ft) tall, are well worth planting.

The echinaceas are best planted in spring. Add leaf-mould or well-rotted compost to the soil at the time of planting. Propagate by seed sown in spring, by root cuttings in autumn, or by division in spring.

Take care
Choose a sunny spot. 66♦

Echinops ritro 'Taplow blue'
(Steel globe thistle)
- **Full sun**
- **Not fussy over soil**
- **Late summer flowering**

Globe thistles have round drumstick heads in varying tones of blue. They are coarse growing; attached to the stout rough wiry stems is deeply cut greyish spiny foliage, woolly beneath. Bees are especially attracted to the globular flowers. The flowerheads can be dried for winter decoration. The variety 'Taplow Blue' is 150cm (5ft) tall, with dark blue globular flowers that have a metallic steely lustre. A variety with a slightly richer blue is 'Veitch's Blue'. There is also the white species *E. nivalis (E. niveus)*. These hardy herbaceous perennials can be grown successfully in the poorest of soils, whether sand or chalk, but should be well drained.

Propagate by root cuttings in late autumn or winter, or by division in autumn or spring.

Take care
Provide a good depth of soil, as the thong-like roots of this plant are very penetrating. 67♦

Erigeron 'Quakeress'

(Fleabane)
- Sunny location
- Not fussy over soil
- Summer flowering

With a pretty name like 'Quakeress', it is unfortunate that this erigeron has the common name 'fleabane'. All the erigerons have a long flowering period, and their daisy-like flowers are in varying shades of blue, pink, mauve or violet. 'Quakeress' has pale blue flowers, and is 60cm (24in) high. Of similar height is 'Charity', a light pink, or 'Darkest of All', a deep violet blue. Where shorter varieties are needed, plant the semi-double light blue 'Prosperity', only 45cm (18in) high, or the very dwarf pink-flowered 'Dimity'.

Erigerons are real sun-lovers, and if they have well-drained soil they will not present any problems. Plant in spring, in batches of five or six plants to each square metre/square yard.

Propagate by seeds sown out of doors in spring, or by division in spring or autumn.

Eryngium bourgatii

(Sea holly)
- Sunny location
- Fertile well-drained soil
- Summer and late summer flowering

As their name implies, the sea hollies have spiny holly-like foliage which is especially attractive, and thistle-like flowerheads in varying shades of blue. They are hardy, and flourish by the sea coast. *E. bourgatii* is a native of the Pyrenees having grey-green foliage and blue-green thistle-like flowers, borne on wiry branching stems. A beautiful evergreen sea holly from Morocco is *E. variifolium.* The spiny toothed rounded leaves are small compared with many eryngiums, and each leaf has distinctive white veins. The flowers, which are not striking, are borne in late summer and carried on erect stems. The British sea holly, *E. maritimum,* has glaucous leaves and charming blue flowers.

Propagate eryngiums by taking root cuttings in late winter or by sowing seed during early spring.

Take care
Avoid waterlogged soil.

Take care
Do not allow these plants to become waterlogged. 67♦

Eupatorium purpureum 'Atropurpureum'

(Joe Pye weed)
- Sunny location
- Any good fertile soil
- Early autumn flowering

This plant has always attracted my attention by its tall handsome upright purplish stems, bedecked with large fluffy branching heads of flowers in varying shades of pale purple, mauve-pink, cinnamon-pink, purplish rose, and purple-lilac. My reason for giving such a list of colours is that much depends on the individual admirer of this 150-180cm (5-6ft) dominating perennial. The variety 'Atropurpureum' has foliage that is purplish, and its fluffy flowers are rosy lilac.

In a large border it needs to be planted well behind shorter-growing plants, or they will be hidden. This North American needs good rich soil if it is to give of its best; a mulch in spring with well-rotted farmyard manure or good garden compost will be welcome. This is an ideal perennial to grow in a wild or semi-wild garden. Propagation is by division in autumn.

Take care
Make sure plants are not starved. 68♦

Euphorbia characias

(Sub-shrubby spurge)
- Sun or shade
- Fertile soil, moderately drained
- Early spring flowering

This evergreen is a sub-species of *E. wulfenii*. Here is a plant which appears in lists of hardy herbaceous perennials although, as I have said, it is an evergreen and therefore its shoots do not die down in winter, as is usually the case with hardy herbaceous perennials. *E. w. characias* has narrow flower spikes that are green with dark brown centres; *E. wulfenii* has broader flower spikes, also green, but with yellowish centres. Their erect stems are about 120cm (4ft) tall, with grey-green glaucous foliage, each stem turning over rather like a shepherd's crook. The following spring each stem is topped by a flowerhead, after which the stems die down to the base and eventually have to be removed.

Propagate by seed or softwood cuttings in spring.

Take care
The white sap from shoots can irritate some skins.

Above: Doronicum 'Miss Mason'
The yellow daisy-like flowers of this lovely hybrid are a welcome sight in spring. Carried on wiry stems up to 45cm (18in) tall, these blooms are excellent for cutting. 61♦

Left: **Echinacea purpurea**
*This hardy perennial is a stately
plant, its richly coloured flowers
appearing in midsummer. It is a
strongly growing subject that will
thrive in sunshine and warmth.* 62♦

Right: **Echinops ritro**
*The globe thistles are coarse, prickly
foliaged plants which in late summer
are festooned with blue globular
flowers about 5cm (2in) across. Easy
to grow in full sun.* 62♦

Below: **Eryngium bourgatii**
*On a fertile well-drained soil this
striking plant will produce its lovely
thistle-like flowers on stems up to
45cm (18in) tall in summer.
Decorative grey-green foliage.* 63♦

Above: **Euphorbia griffithii 'Fireglow'**
This plant produces red-tipped shoots from the base that gradually develop into attractive green foliage which, in early summer, is enhanced by striking orange-red bracts. 81♦

Left: **Eupatorium purpureum 'Atropurpureum'**
The purplish foliage of this pretty variety is an added bonus to the autumnal rose-lilac flowers. 64♦

Right: **Festuca glauca**
This densely tufted perennial grass is a useful plant for the front of the border. It will thrive in sun. 81♦

Above: **Galega officinalis**
Galegas have a sprawling habit and are best planted near the back of the border. Small pea-shaped blooms are borne on branching stems. 83♦

Right: **Filipendula purpurea**
A splendid plant for a cool moist spot. The handsome foliage is crowned with lovely carmine-rose flowers on stems 60-120cm (2-4ft) high. 82♦

Below: **Galtonia candicans**
Once established this bulbous plant will produce fragrant white blooms in late summer. Plant the bulbs 15cm (6in) deep in fertile soil. 84♦

Left: **Gentiana asclepiadea**
This is a most attractive gentian with glossy green willow-like leaves and rich blue flowers in the early autumn. Partial shade and moist conditions suit this plant best. Leave undisturbed to naturalize. 84♦

Right: **Gypsophila paniculata**
A magnificent display of feathery white flowers covers this plant in midsummer. It is deep-rooted and needs well-prepared soil and full sunshine to become established. 87♦

Below:
Helenium autumnale 'Wyndley'
The heleniums enrich the garden with bright daisy-like flowers in shades of yellow and orange. This lovely variety has large coppery-yellow blooms on erect stems. 87♦

73

Left: **Helianthus decapetalus**
*The perennial sunflowers produce
large daisy-like flowers on stout
stems up to 150cm (5ft) in height.
They are vigorous plants.* 88▶

Right: **Helleborus corsicus**
*Clusters of fascinating pale green
cup-shaped flowers are produced by
this plant from winter until early
spring. The three-lobed leaves make
a handsome display on their own.* 89▶

Below:
Hemerocallis 'Pink Damask'
*The beautiful pink lily-like blooms of
this recommended variety are
carried on stems up to 75cm (30in) in
height. Allow these superb plants to
grow undisturbed in good soil.* 90▶

Above: **Heuchera sanguinea 'Red Spangles'**
This is one of the best varieties to grow; its blood-red bell-shaped flowers are borne on slender stems up to 50cm (20in) in height. 91♦

Right: **Hosta rectifolia 'Tall Boy'**
A lovely hybrid for the border. 92♦

Below: **Hosta fortunei 'Albopicta Aurea'**
Grown for its stunning foliage. 92♦

Above: **Iberis sempervirens**
*This half-shrubby perennial is an
ideal edging plant. Its dark evergreen
foliage forms hummocks that are
covered with white flowers in spring
and early summer.* 92♦

Left: **Inula helenium**
*A hardy herbaceous perennial with
many deep yellow daisy-like blooms
carried single on wiry stems above a
dense display of narrow leaves. It
thrives in a moist spot.* 93♦

Right: **Incarvillea mairei**
*Beautiful pink-purple flowers with
yellow throats adorn this plant in
early summer. It grows to 30cm
(12in) in height and so is ideal for the
front of a sunny border.* 93♦

Above:
Iris sibirica 'Heavenly Blue'
The rich blue flowers are carried two *or three to a stem up to 120cm (4ft)* *above the grassy sword-like foliage.* *Provide ample moisture.* 95♦

Euphorbia griffithii 'Fireglow'

(Spurge)
- **Sun or partial shade**
- **Good fertile soil**
- **Early summer flowering**

E. griffithii has bright yellow flowers 45cm (18in) high; it was introduced from the Himalayas, and was first exhibited in 1954. The flowerheads of 'Fireglow' are a rich burnt orange shade (frequently described as brick red), and carried on erect stems. My own plant has not flowered so far and I am anxiously looking forward to it blooming, when its 75cm (30in) stems will carry their handsome coloured 'flowers', which are in fact bracts.

'Fireglow' does best in an open sunny spot or partial shade. It has slow-spreading shoots, which appear around the base. The dull red asparagus-like shoots soon develop into dark green foliage, reddish beneath.

Propagate this plant by division in spring or autumn.

Take care
Its roots may become invasive, but if you admire it you will probably not mind. 68-9▸

Festuca glauca

(Sheep's fescue)
- **Sunny location**
- **Well-drained soil**
- **Midsummer flowering**

This useful and accommodating grass is a form of sheep's fescue, *Festuca ovina. F. glauca* is a densely tufted perennial, with little plumes like miniature pampas grass. The neat clumps have flower spikes 23-25cm (9-10in) tall. It is an ideal plant for the front of a border or as an edging. The foliage is steely blue-grey or a glaucous grey. As it is a slow grower it does not require replanting for several years. Other fescues are *F. amethystina,* which has stems of powder blue 23cm (9in) tall, and *F. punctoria,* which is a steely blue and only 15cm (6in) high.

All these fescues like full sun and are at their best on dry soils. Propagate them by sowing seeds in spring or by division in early autumn or spring.

Take care
Plant in early autumn or spring, and always in light well-drained soil. 69▸

Filipendula purpurea
(Dropwort)
- **Sun or partial shade**
- **Cool moist conditions**
- **Summer flowering**

This Japanese hardy herbaceous perennial is one of half a dozen dropworts. It can still be found in some nursery catalogues and garden centres under its old name, *Spiraea palmatum*. This is a most handsome plant, and if it has moist soil or is growing near the side of a pond, it will not fail to attract attention. It has large lobed leaves and above the elegant leafy crimson stems are large flat heads bearing many tiny carmine-rose flowers, each stem reaching a height of 60-120cm (2-4ft). The pinkish *F. rubra* has large flowerheads up to 28cm (11in) across. In damp soil it will form huge clumps, in either sun or shade.

To obtain the best results, grow this plant in partial shade and in rich fertile moist soil. Propagate by seeds sown in pans or boxes under glass in autumn, or by division in autumn.

Take care
Make sure that this plant does not lack moisture. 71▶

Francoa sonchifolia
(Bridal wreath)
- **Sun or partial shade**
- **Any well-drained soil**
- **Summer flowering**

The best-known bridal wreath is *F. racemosa*, which needs to be grown indoors. The so-called half-hardy *F. sonchifolia* is much hardier. It is a graceful plant, and the long erect wand-like stems rise 45-60cm (18-24in) above the deeply lobed dark green foliage. At the top of these wands are carried numerous heads of white and deep pink flowers with red spots at the base of each petal. The flowers are long lasting, and even when over they look quite attractive at first, but as winter draws near they are best cut down.

Grow *F. sonchifolia* in any well-drained soil in a sunny position or one providing partial shade. The lovely flowers are produced in midsummer.

Propagate by seed sown in spring under glass, or by division in spring.

Take care
Choose a sheltered spot and plant in spring for best results.

Gaillardia aristata

(Blanket flower)
- **Sunny location**
- **Light well-drained soil**
- **Summer flowering**

The gaillardias are among the most colourful perennials, and the hybrids are chiefly derived from *G. aristata*, better known in the nursery trade as *G. grandiflora*. These vivid flowers can be had in shades of yellow, bronze, orange, flame, brown and maroon-red. Their large daisy-like saucer-shaped flowers are ideal for cutting. The height varies from 60-90cm (2-3ft). All parts of the plant are sticky, and its soft leaves have an aromatic scent.

As they are short-lived, gaillardias should be grown in well-drained soil, and they will flourish in calcareous soils, ie chalk or lime. Fortunately, they grow with the minimum of attention; the long flowering season lasts from mid to late summer.

Propagate by seeds sown under glass in late winter or out of doors in early summer, or by root cuttings in autumn or softwood cuttings in midsummer.

Take care
As gaillardias are rather floppy, support them with a few peasticks.

Galega officinalis

(Goat's rue)
- **Full sun**
- **Any good soil, or even poor soils**
- **Summer flowering**

This is a perennial that needs to be at the back of the border, as it has a rather sprawling habit, so plant it behind perennials that can shield it when the flowers have faded and the plant is looking a little the worse for wear. What a joy goat's rue is, as it will thrive in any sunny corner and in any good soil. The small pea-shaped flowers of *G. officinalis* are mauve, and they are borne on branching stems up to 150cm (5ft) tall. As a contrast to *G. officinalis* there is an attractive white variety called 'Candida'.

Plant galegas in autumn or early spring and allow sufficient room for them to develop. They will thrive in a sunny location and are generally free of pests and diseases.

Propagate by division in autumn or spring.

Take care
Insert a few peasticks in the ground early in the year, so that the plants can grow through to hide them. 70♦

83

Galtonia candicans

(Summer hyacinth; Spire lily;
Cape hyacinth)
- **Full sun**
- **Deep fertile soil**
- **Late summer flowering**

This liliaceous bulb has fragrant
white dangling bell-like flowers
carried on 90-120cm (3-4ft) stout
tube-like stems; at the base are long
glaucous-green leaves.

This bulb has to be planted 15cm
(6in) below the soil, which needs to
be well drained. Bulbs can be
planted in autumn or spring, and in a
year or so they will be established. If
they are planted behind the violet-
flowered liriope, the two may flower
together. This bulb needs good
fertile soil, as bulbs may deteriorate
in poor sandy soil. Once established
they should be left undisturbed.
Propagate by detaching offsets in
spring, but not too often. Seeds
can be sown as soon as ripe out of
doors, or under glass in spring.
Galtonia will readily produce self-
sown seedlings.

Take care
Add plenty of humus, such as well-
rotted farmyard manure or well-
rotted garden compost, before
planting bulbs. 70♦

Gentiana asclepiadea

(Willow gentian)
- **Shade or partial shade**
- **Rich moist soil**
- **Early autumn flowering**

This European charmer has graceful
stems and willow-like foliage. The
arching stems, 45-60cm (18-24in)
long, carry glossy leaves, and pairs
of azure-blue to almost bluish purple
tubular flowers, singly in the axils of
the leaves, in the early autumn.

To get the best from this plant it
needs dappled sunlight in woodland,
but if a really moist soil is available,
even a chalk soil, the willow gentian
can be grown. It does need a rich
moist soil containing a good
proportion of humus, such as rotted
leaf-mould. Once established, plants
will seed themselves and become
naturalized.

Propagate by seed, sown as soon
as it is ripe: the seedlings will take at
least two years before they flower.
Alternatively, propagate by division
in spring.

Take care
Plant firmly, and in spring. 72♦

Geranium 'Johnson's Blue'

(Cranesbill)
- **Sunny location**
- **Fertile well-drained soil**
- **Early summer flowering**

This geranium is a most captivating plant. Above the elegantly divided foliage that covers the ground, the wiry 30-35cm (12-14in) stems carry lavender-blue cup-shaped flowers with darker veins. The flowers are produced profusely from early summer onwards; each measures up to 5cm (2in) across. A second flush of these lovely blooms can be encouraged by cutting down old flowering stems. A border of this plant in front of a hedge of white floribunda roses looks really stunning.

Provided this and other geraniums have good ordinary soil and good drainage, very little else is needed. Plant in autumn or spring, five plants to the square metre/square yard. Protect young plants from the ravages of slugs. Propagate by division of roots in autumn or spring.

Take care
Give geraniums good drainage.

Geranium macrorrhizum

(Large-rooted cranesbill)
- **Sun or partial shade**
- **Well-drained soil**
- **Late spring flowering**

This woody rooted cranesbill is a perfect ground cover. The palmate five-lobed leaves, over 5cm (2in) across, are light green or dull purplish-crimson, clammy to the touch and aromatic; in mild winters they are semi-evergreen. When growing in well-drained poorish soil, the leaves become very decorative in autumn. The leaves are a light purple crimson underneath. The flowers are white stained with pink, and appear freely in early summer. The flower stalks are 30cm (12in) high, with several blooms on each stalk. It is from the aromatic foliage of this geranium that the oil of geranium in commerce is extracted.

Propagate by seed sown in early spring under glass, or by division in autumn or spring.

Take care
Clear the ground of any pernicious weeds, for once geraniums are established, it is difficult to weed them effectively.

Geum chiloense
(Scarlet avens)
- **Sun or partial shade**
- **Good fertile soil**
- **Early summer flowering**

Gillenia trifoliata
(Indian physic)
- **Sun or partial shade**
- **Moist fertile soil**
- **Summer flowering**

This is probably the parent of the double red 60cm (24in) variety 'Mrs Bradshaw' and the double yellow 'Lady Stratheden' of similar height. These two geums have wild-rose-like flowers on fairly stiff wiry stems, and dull green strawberry-like foliage. The quite separate hybrid 'Borisii' is not so tall, having 30cm (12in) stems, and above clumps of rich green roundish hairy foliage are single rich orange-red flowers. *G. rivale* 'Leonard's Variety' is also only 30cm (12in) high, and bears on hairy red stems its drooping sprays of deep red calyces surrounded by pinkish brown petals.

These hardy perennials will grow in almost any soil, provided it is not too dry. Propagate them by division, but cut away any pieces that are woody.

Among hardy herbaceous perennials this one must rate quite high, for it is an elegant plant. The 60cm (24in) or more slender reddish stems carry bunches of small white strap-like flowers forming an open star; the flowers are not unlike those of a spiraea or astilbe. The white flowers are backed with wine-red calyces, and the latter remain on the flower stalks long after the white petals have dropped. The flower sprays are suitable for cutting and can be easily arranged. It is quite hardy and easily grown; it prefers a moist peaty soil and partial shade, but will tolerate sun.

Propagate by division in either early autumn or early spring. Seed can be used, but it is a very slow process.

Take care
Divide geums every two or three years, and replant only the youngest pieces.

Take care
Plant in spring, as they need enrichment in the soil; well-rotted garden compost is satisfactory.

Gypsophila paniculata

(Chalk plant; Baby's breath)
- **Sunny location**
- **Well-drained, preferably limy soil**
- **Summer flowering**

The flowerheads of *G. paniculata* are a mass of small feathery flowers, white or pink. The glaucous leaves are also small. The branching flowerheads are used by flower arrangers to add a light cloud effect to arrangements of other flowers. *G. paniculata* 'Bristol Fairy' is the best double form, 90cm (3ft) tall.

As gypsophilas are deep-rooted, the ground must be well prepared before planting; it should be bastard trenched, ie double dug. To do this, take out the first spit or spade's depth of soil, break up the bottom spit with a fork and fill up with the next top spit. Also enrich the ground with well-rotted farmyard manure or well-rotted garden compost. Provided they have full sun and well-drained soil, gypsophilas should be no trouble.

Propagate 'Bristol Fairy' by taking softwood cuttings in late spring to very early summer.

Take care
Insert a few peasticks for support. 73♦

Helenium autumnale 'Wyndley'

(Sneezeweed)
- **Full sun**
- **Prefers heavy soil**
- **Late summer flowering**

The North American helenium is one of those perennials with daisy-like flowers, chiefly in late summer and autumn. The variety 'Wyndley' has large coppery yellow, flecked flowers, 60cm (24in) tall and fairly rigid. Like all helenium flowers, they have a prominent central disc. The 50cm (20in) 'Crimson Beauty' has brownish-red flowers.

Although these plants will grow in almost any type of soil, they prefer a fairly stiff loam. The fact that their stems are fairly rigid can make plants flop over in heavy rain so push in a few peasticks around the plant at an early stage; then the stems will grow through and cover the sticks. Their pleasing branching stems make heleniums useful as cut flowers, and they last well in water.

Propagate heleniums by softwood cuttings in early summer, or by division in autumn or spring.

Take care
Keep moist during hot dry spells in summer. 72-3♦

Helianthus decapetalus

(Sunflower)
- **Full sun**
- **Well-drained stiff loam**
- **Late summer flowering**

H. decapetalus, from North America, is probably the species from which we have gained several good hybrid sunflowers. All have coarse, rough foliage. The double-flowered 'Loddon Gold' bears rich yellow blossoms on 150cm (5ft) stout stems. The semi-double 'Triomphe de Gand' has large golden-yellow flowers with ball-shaped centres, 120-150cm (4-5ft) high. Another rich yellow variety, 'Morning Sun', has anemone-centred flowers, and this erect and sturdy grower is 120cm (4ft) tall. The graceful, lemon-yellow single-flowered *H. orgyalis* 'Lemon Queen', reaches 150cm (5ft) high.

Grow these plants in a well-drained loamy soil and ensure that they receive plenty of sunshine.

Propagate perennial sunflowers by division in autumn or spring. Divide and replant every three or four years.

Take care
Do not let perennial sunflowers starve; they are greedy feeders. 74♦

Helichrysum angustifolium

(Curry plant)
- **Full sun**
- **Poor well-drained soil**
- **Mid-summer flowering**

This is a hardy evergreen perennial or sub-shrub, but it usually appears in authoritative works on border perennials. The common name curry plant is most descriptive; on a hot day, if it is brushed against, a wonderful aroma of curry fills the air. In spring the foliage is bright silver. This tarnishes as the summer advances, but even in winter it is still a delightful plant, reaching a height of 35cm (14in) and a width of 45-60cm (18-24in).

In midsummer it bears flat terminal crowded heads of small yellow flowers. To prevent it flowering use the shears on the plant as soon as the flower shoots push their way through the silver foliage. This will encourage a fresh batch of young foliage. Propagate in summer by taking half-ripe cuttings with a heel.

Take care
Avoid cold wet soil.

Heliopsis scabra

(Orange sunflower)
- **Full sun**
- **Good fertile soil**
- **Late summer flowering**

Despite its common name, this hardy herbaceous perennial is not a sunflower. It is a stiff upright plant and normally no staking is required. It has strong woody branching stems, and the spear-shaped foliage is dark green; stems and foliage are very rough. Several single or double, yellow or orange flowers, 7.5-10cm (3-4in) across, are carried on each stem. They are very resistant to drought, but will grow in moist or rich soil and become very lush. They flower from midsummer to early autumn.

The perfectly shaped 'Light of Loddon' has anemone centred bright yellow flowers 105-120cm (42-48in) high; it is free flowering and if cut in the evening blooms will last well in water.

Propagate by division, or by basal cuttings in spring.

Take care
Cut down flowering stems to ground level in late autumn.

Helleborus corsicus

(Corsican hellebore)
- **Partial shade or some sun**
- **Well-drained fertile retentive soil**
- **Winter and spring flowering**

This native of the Balearic Islands, Corsica and Sardinia is an outstanding and lovely hellebore, which has been known as *H. argutifolius* and *H. lividus corsicus*. Here is a perennial worth waiting for after it is first planted. It is a bushy plant, 60cm (24in) tall, with tripartite leathery glaucous leaves with spined tipped edges. Above its handsome foliage are clusters of pale green cup-like drooping flowers, with centres of pale green stamens; the flowers last for many months, from winter well into spring, but unfortunately, they do not make successful cut flowers.

Propagate by seeds sown in spring or autumn, or by division of the roots in spring.

Take care
Remove old stems as they die, cutting each stem back almost to ground level. 75♦

Helleborus orientalis

(Lenten rose)
- Partial or full shade
- Not fussy over soil, provided it is not bog
- Winter and spring flowering

This native of Greece and Asia Minor has produced a large number of good garden varieties in many colours, including pure white, cream, green, pink, rose, purple, plum-colour or almost black, and prettily spotted maroon or crimson. They are 45cm (18in) tall, and have large open cup-like flowers. The foliage is evergreen, and once established they act as very useful ground cover.

The variety 'Kochii' is a little shorter than *H. orientalis* and blooms a little earlier, having large coarsely toothed foliage; in bud it is yellowish green, later opening its nodding primrose-yellow flowers.

Provided the soil is fertile and the plants are growing in partial or full shade, they should give pleasure for many years. Propagate by seeds sown in spring or autumn, or by division of the roots in spring.

Take care
These hellebores do not make good cut flowers.

Hemerocallis

(Day lily)
- Sun or partial shade
- Any soil but avoid dry ones
- Summer flowering

The day lilies are hardy, the large clumps producing an abundance of bright green arching foliage and a display of scented lily-like flowers over a long period. The flowers of early day lilies lasted for only one day, but modern varieties last two or sometimes three days. The lily-like flowers are carried at the top of stout 90cm (36in) stems.

Three modern varieties are: 'Pink Damask', with pretty pink flowers, 75cm (30in); 'Nashville', large, creamy yellow with streaked orange-red throat markings, 90cm (36in); and the glowing bright red 'Stafford', 75cm (30in).

Propagate day lilies by division in spring. Plants can be left undisturbed for many years; lifting and divide them only when clumps become overcrowded.

Take care
In very hot dry weather, give plants a thorough soaking. 74-5▶

Hesperis matronalis

(Sweet rocket; Dame's violet)
- **Sun or partial shade**
- **Well-drained moist soil**
- **Summer flowering**

The single hesperis is not a long-lived perennial, and it is therefore necessary to raise fresh stock. Single seed is available in shades of lilac, purple and white. As a cut flower choose the double white. The singles are easier to grow than the doubles. Plants are 105-120cm (42-48in) in height. The cross-shaped blooms develop on spikes up to 45cm (18in) long in midsummer and are sweetly fragrant during the evening. Once they have finished flowering it is best to cut the flower spikes down.

To be successful, hesperis needs good drainage and a moist sandy loam. Propagate the singles as biennials, sowing seed out of doors in spring; the double varieties can be divided in spring, or cuttings of basal growth taken in midsummer or early autumn. However, singles will seed themselves about, once established.

Take care
Seek doubles, but at least try the singles.

Heuchera sanguinea 'Red Spangles'

(Coral bells)
- **Sun or partial shade**
- **Well-drained fertile soil**
- **Early summer flowering**

Heucheras have evergreen heart-shaped leaves and their pretty tiny bell-shaped flowers hang down from slender wiry stems. The foliage comes in various shades of green, sometimes with zonal markings marbled like pelargoniums. 'Red Spangles' has crimson-scarlet flowers and is 50cm (20in) tall.

Heucheras make bold clumps as much as 30cm (12in) wide, but deteriorate if not divided and transplanted every few years; throw out woody pieces, keeping only the young vigorous ones. Work in well-rotted garden compost or well-rotted manure before planting. Heucheras prefer a light, well-drained fertile soil, but dislike cold clay, wet or very acid soils. Given good feeding, flowers will be produced from spring to early autumn. Propagate by division in late summer or early autumn.

Take care
Keep moist during hot dry days in the summer. 76♦

91

Hosta fortunei 'Albopicta'
(Plaintain lily)
- Dense or partial shade
- Rich fertile soil
- Summer flowering

The hosta, previously called *Funkia*, has become popular since the second World War, because the large and beautiful foliage is used for flower arrangements. 'Albopicta' has large scrolled leaves exquisitely marbled in shades of golden yellow and edged with pale green. As summer advances the golden yellow becomes primrose coloured and the pale green turns darker. Above this magnificent foliage are 45-60cm (18-24in) stems carrying bell-like flowers. A recent introduction is *H. rectifolia* 'Tall Boy' with green leaves and violet-mauve flowers.

Provided hostas are not allowed to become dry during summer, and are well laced with rotted farmyard manure or well-rotted garden compost, the gardener will be rewarded handsomely for his labours. Propagate these plants by division in spring.

Take care
Do not let hostas become dry. 76-7♦

Iberis sempervirens
(Perennial candytuft)
- Full sun
- Any soil
- Spring and early summer flowering

This is half-shrubby, but a superb plant to grow either as an edging to a path or as a bold clump. Even when it is not in flower, its bright to darkish evergreen foliage looks attractive. In spring and early summer the mounds of evergreen foliage are covered with dense wreaths of snowy white flowers; the hummocks of green are about 30cm (12in) high.

Provided they grow in good soil, plants will flourish for a number of years. After flowering has finished, cut off the old flowerheads; this encourages new growth and keeps the tufts neat and tidy. Propagate by taking half-ripe cuttings during early summer, inserting them in a cold frame or under a large glass jar.

Take care
The ground where iberis is to be planted should be free of perennial weeds, as it is difficult to eradicate such weeds once the plants are established. 78♦

Incarvillea mairei

(Trumpet flower)
- **Full sun**
- **Light fertile soil**
- **Early summer flowering**

This handsome perennial,
sometimes known as *Incarvillea
grandiflora brevipes*, is 30cm (12in)
tall, with deeply pinnate foliage. The
flowers, held well above the foliage,
are a rich pinkish purple, with a
yellow throat.

 The fleshy root needs to be
planted 7.5cm (3in) deep.
Incarvilleas need a light sandy well-
drained soil in full sun. As this
species is only 30cm (12in) high, it
needs to be planted near the front of
the border. In gardens where frost
could cause damage, put a covering
of bracken or a pane of glass over
these plants during the winter.

 Propagate by sowing seed as
soon as possible after ripening.
Although division can be done in
spring, the crowns may be too tough
to split easily and so seed is perhaps
a wiser way to increase them.

Take care
As slugs are attracted by incarvilleas,
put down slug pellets. 79♦

Inula helenium

(Elecampane)
- **Sunny location**
- **Moist soil**
- **Summer flowering**

The inulas are showy sun-loving
hardy herbaceous perennials with
brightly coloured daisy-like flowers.
Although they can be grown in the
herbaceous border they are really
more at home in a moist situation,
beside the margin of a pond or
stream.

 I. helenium reaches a height of
90-120cm (3-4ft), it has bright yellow
flowers similar to small sunflowers,
and large leaves. A real beauty
(when it can be obtained) is *I.
royleana*, with yellow rayed flowers,
10-12cm (4-4.75in) wide, on 60cm
(24in) stems; this species must have
moisture. Two other varieties are *I.
ensifolia* 'Compacta', with golden
rayed flowers on stems 25cm (10in)
high and *I. ensifolia* 'Golden Beauty',
which is 60cm (24in) high, and has
golden flowers that last for weeks.

 Propagate inulas by seed sown in
spring, or by division in autumn or
spring.

Take care
Do not let the soil dry out. 78♦

Iris sibirica 'Heavenly Blue'

(Siberian iris)
- **Sunny location**
- **Moist soil, but tolerates dry**
- **Early summer flowering**

These irises give of their best when the soil is moist; they can make a colourful display under drier conditions, but do not grow so tall. All varieites of Siberian iris have grassy sword-like leaves and strong straight slender stems, varying in height from 60-120cm (2-4ft). Each head carries two or three flowers. 'Heavenly Blue', a pretty rich azure blue, is 120cm (4ft) tall.

This species is easily raised from seed but, as there is such a variety to select from, it is better to choose the colours and plant them in clumps of three. Grow them in a sunny position where their roots are moist. Unlike the flag irises, these do not need lime. The brown seedpods, which last through the winter, are attractive in the border as well as in flower arrangements indoors.

Propagate by division in early autumn or late spring.

Take care
These irises need an ample supply of moisture for best results. 80♦

Iris unguicularis

(Algerian iris)
- **Full sun**
- **Well-drained soil**
- **Winter flowering**

This winter-flowering iris, known for many years as *I. stylosa,* is more correctly *I. unguicularis*. The lilac-lavender flowers are prettily veined, on 30cm (12in) stems, and the abundant glossy foliage is 60cm (24in) long.

This plant needs a poor dry soil. Choose a sunny well-drained site and plant in autumn – not in spring, as often advised – because the roots need plenty of moisture, which they can get from autumn and winter rains. In autumn cut back the foliage on established plants to about 15-20cm (6-8in) from ground level. Pull out dead leaves, using leather gloves, as the leaves can cut. Give a spring dressing of the following, all by weight: 4 parts superphosphate of lime; 2 parts sulphate of ammonia; and 1 part sulphate of potash. Apply this at 85gm (3oz) per square metre/yard. In early summer apply 57gm (2oz) of magnesium sulphate per square metre/yard. Propagate by division in autumn.

Take care
Choose a hot sunny site.

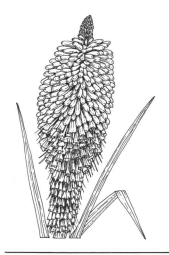 

Kniphofia

((Red hot poker; Torch lily)
- **Full sun**
- **Rich retentive well-drained soil**
- **Early summer to autumn flowering**

Kniphofias will come through most winters. To ensure their safety, tie the foliage into a kind of wigwam in winter, to keep the crowns dry. The flowers are carried on stout stems; one beauty is 'Little Maid' about 60cm (24in) tall, with attractive creamy flower spikes. *K. galpinii* 'Bressingham Seedlings' produce graceful spikes in orange shades, 45-90cm (18-36in) tall, through summer to autumn. *Kniphofia praecox* has brilliant scarlet flowers on 180-210cm (6-7ft) stems.

Kniphofias require a fairly rich soil with ample humus such as rotted manure or garden compost. After clumps have been divided, do not allow them to dry out before or after planting. A mulch of rotted manure or garden compost should be given annually in spring; otherwise they can remain untouched for several years. Plant them three or four to the square metre/yard. Propagate by division in spring.

Take care
Protect crowns during winter. 97, 98♦

Lathyrus latifolius

(Perennial pea)
- **Sunny location**
- **Good fertile soil**
- **Summer to early autumn flowering**

Large sheets of bloom of the perennial pea can often be seen along railway embankments. It is excellent for planting beside a wire fence, on trellis or supported by a few peasticks. The flowers are rosy pink to reddish purple; there is also a good white form, 'White Pearl', and 'Rose queen' has pink flowers with a white eye. Sprays of flowers arranged in pairs are carried on the end of stiff stems. Perennial peas bloom throughout the summer until early autumn; the flowers are useful for cutting for indoor decoration. Plants are 150-165cm (5-5.5ft) in height.

These plants enjoy a well-enriched soil. Propagate them by seed sown in spring, or by division of the roots in spring. Be sure to protect seedlings and young plants from slugs, which can cause serious damage to stems and leaves.

Take care
Insert peasticks early in the season.

Lavatera olbia 'Rosea'

(Tree mallow)
- Full sun
- Well-drained fertile soil
- Summer and autumn flowering

The tree mallow is a woody plant and correctly classed as a sub-shrub, but it is usually grown in hardy flower borders. It grows especially well in coastal areas where frost is not a problem. Plants reach a height of 150cm (5ft) and as much in width, so they should be placed in a border where they will not overshadow other plants. The large hollyhock-like flowers of a deep old-rose pink are profusely borne on branching woody stems. The vine-like foliage is a dull green.

This species needs a rich well-drained soil. Always have young stock plants. Once frosts are past, cut back all young growth annually to near the base. Propagate by seeds sown in spring under glass, or by half-ripe cuttings in summer.

Liatris spicata 'Kobold'

(Spike gayfeather)
- Full sun
- Ordinary well-drained soil
- Summer flowering

The flowers of liatris open at the top first, whereas most plants that have spike-like flowers open from the base, and those at the top open last. The small strap-like leaves form a rosette near the ground; the flower stems also have small leaves. The flowerheads are closely packed and look not unlike a paint brush. The variety 'Kobold' has brilliant pinky mauve flowers, 60cm (24in) tall. Also recommended is *L. pycnostachya*, the Kansas feather, with pinky purple crowded flowerheads, 15-20cm (6-8in) long, on rather floppy 120cm (4ft) stems. It makes a fine display in late summer and early autumn. Liatris are useful as cut flowers and ideal for drying for winter flower arrangements.

The species is better in poor soil, and prefers firm ground. Propagate by seed sown in pans in early spring, or by division in late spring.

Take care
Keep plants in good shape by annual pruning. 98♦

Take care
Do not grow liatris in rich soil. 99♦

Above: **Kniphofia 'Little Maid'**
*This is a particularly attractive variety
to grow; its creamy white blooms are*
60cm (24in) tall and excellent for
cutting. Grow these plants in a well-
drained soil. 95♦

Left: **Kniphofia praecox**
This is a tall variety – up to 210cm (7ft) tall – with magnificent spikes of tubular crimson flowers that make a fine display in late summer and early autumn. 95♦

Right: **Liatris spicata 'Kobold'**
The frothy flowers of the liatris have the unusual habit of opening from the top downwards. This lovely variety has pink-purple flower spikes that can be cut for indoors. 96♦

Below: **Lavatera olbia 'Rosea'**
This is a shrubby perennial that grows up to 150cm (5ft) tall with attractive pink flowers in summer and early autumn. Pruning in spring will keep the plant in good shape. 96♦

Left: **Lobelia 'Cherry Ripe'**
This is one of the best of the many hybrids of Lobelia cardinalis *and* L. fulgens. *Its bright cerise-scarlet flowers appear in late summer on stems up to 120cm (4ft) tall.* 115♦

Right: **Liriope muscari**
A hardy evergreen perennial with arching grass-like foliage that forms a neat hummock in the border. In late summer and autumn erect stems of lilac-mauve blooms appear. 114♦

Below: **Lunaria rediviva**
The perennial form of the popular plant 'honesty' bears pretty lilac to lavender flowers in spring and flat papery seedpods that can be used for indoor decoration. 115♦

Above: **Lupinus polyphyllus 'Russell Hybrids'**
The Russel lupins provide a good mixture of colours for the garden on stems up to 120cm (4ft) tall. Grow these on acid or neutral soil. 116♦

Left: **Lychnis coronaria 'Abbotswood Rose'**
Branching sprays of rose-crimson flowers adorn this plant during the summer. The silvery foliage is an excellent foil to the blooms. 116♦

Right: **Lysimachia punctata**
In moist situations this vigorous perennial will provide a long display of bright yellow flowers during the summer. It grows 90cm (3ft) tall and will tolerate semi-shade 117♦

Above: Macleaya microcarpa
An imposing perennial that should be given ample room to spread. The branching plumes of buff or flesh tinted flowers reach a height of about 240cm (8ft) in late summer. 118♦

Left: Lythrum salicaria 'Firecandle'
Handsome spikes of deep rosy red flowers adorn this dependable plant in late summer. It will thrive in moist retentive garden soils. 117♦

Right: Malva moschata 'Alba'
This pure white form of the musk mallow is a lovely perennial with flowering stems 75cm (30in) tall. It is short lived but self-sown seedlings are always plentiful. 118♦

Above: **Monarda didyma
'Cambridge Scarlet'**
*Both the foliage and flowers of this
summer-blooming perennial are
fragrant. Grow it in sun or partial
shade and be sure to keep it moist.* 120♦

Left: **Melianthus major**
*An evergreen sub-shrub grown for
its large, deeply serrated leaves. It is
best suited to mild areas and must
have protection against frost to
survive. Ideal for poor soils.* 119♦

Below: **Myrrhis odorata**
*This delightful herb has aromatic
fern-like foliage and creamy white
flowers in early summer. As autumn
approaches the leaves turn red. A
useful, dependable plant.* 121♦

Left: **Nepeta × faassenii**
Excellent for edging and beneath roses, this charming plant has aromatic foliage irresistible to cats and lovely sprays of lavender-blue flowers for many weeks during the summer. Grow in full sun. 121♦

Right: **Onopordon acanthium**
Although strictly a biennial, this impressive thistle is usually grown in the herbaceous border. Stems can be 210cm (7ft) tall, with grey foliage and attractive purple flowers. 122♦

Below: **Oenothera missouriensis**
A superb ground cover plant with dark green narrow leaves that hug the ground and red-spotted bright yellow flowers borne on red stems 23cm (9in) high. It must have a freely draining soil to succeed. 122♦

Above: **Paeonia officinalis 'Rubra Plena'**
This old favourite among peonies has large heads of double crimson blooms on stems up to 60cm (24in) tall. Best left undisturbed. 124▸

Above: **Osmunda regalis**
A noble fern that thrives in partial shade and moist conditions. Lovely yellow and russet autumn hues. 123♦

Below: **Papaver orientale**
Unsurpassed for their large colourful blooms, the Oriental poppies thrive in a well-drained sunny location. 124♦

Above: **Phlomis russeliana**
Whorls of rich yellow hooded flowers are borne on stately spikes up to *90cm (3ft) above the heart-shaped basal leaves. The seedheads are ideal for indoor decoration.* 126♦

Libertia formosa

- **Full sun**
- **Well-drained fertile soil**
- **Summer flowering**

This evergreen perennial from Chile is not hardy in the coldest areas, but in a sunny sheltered situation it will come through most winters. It has attractive dark green sword-shaped foliage forming dense tufts from which arise 75cm (30in) stems. During summer it bears sprays of ivory-white saucer-shaped flowers, enhanced by a boss of yellow stamens. In autumn orange-brown seedheads are produced. *L. grandiflora* and *L. ixioides* also have foliage that turns an attractive orange-brown in winter.

Libertias must have well-drained soil; add moistened peat, leaf-mould and sharp sand when preparing the ground for planting in spring. Propagate by seeds sown as soon as ripe, in late summer to early autumn, or by dividing the fibrous roots in spring.

Take care
Provide good drainage, and ample moisture in summer.

Ligularia 'Gregynog Gold'

(Golden groundsel)
- **Full sun or partial shade**
- **Moist conditions**
- **Late summer to early autumn flowering**

This handsome perennial is a hybrid between *L. dentata* and *L. vietchianus*. Above its large handsome heart-shaped leaves, up to 30cm (12in) across, arise stout stems 60-90cm (24-36in) high, on top of which are erect spike-like flower sprays up to 7.5cm (3in) across. The magnificent blooms are a beautiful orange-gold with bronzy maroon discs and prettily freckled with yellow. The flowers look partiuclarly attractive when seen in autumn sunshine. This fine hybrid, known for almost 50 years, deserves to be more popular.

This ligularia does best when growing in moist soil, in a boggy situation beside a pool or stream. Propagate it by division in spring.

Take care
Keep plants moist.

Linaria purpurea
(Purple toadflax)
- **Full sun or partial shade**
- **Well-drained soil**
- **All summer flowering**

This S European perennial may
become a weed, but when properly
understood it will be appreciated for
its long season of flowering. Its small
antirrhinum-like flowers are carried
on thin wiry stems, and it has greyish
narrow leaves. The blooms are a
lovely purple-blue with a beard
of white. An excellent garden
variety is 'Canon Went', with bright
pink flowers that have an orange spot
on the lip of each flower. Both *L.
purpurea* and the variety 'Canon
Went' grow 60-90cm (24-36in) tall.
No staking is necessary. Plants will
thrive in a well-drained soil and will
tolerate sun or semi-shade.

Linaria seeds itself freely, yet it is
easy enough to cull unwanted plants.
Propagate by sowing seeds in late
spring out of doors, or by division in
spring.

Liriope muscari
(Turf lily)
- **Sunny location**
- **Fertile soil with moderate
drainage**
- **Late summer or autumn
flowering**

As its name suggests, *L. muscari* is
not unlike an outsize grape hyacinth.
Its foliage arches over, forming a
neat hummock from which the 23-
30cm (9-12in) stems arise, bearing
lilac-mauve flowers crowded
together and looking rather like a
bottle brush. I have seen liriope used
most effectively as an edging to a
border of shrubs; it is always useful
to have a few of these evergreen
plants in a border during winter.

Having grown liriope in a clay soil
with a pH 6.5 reading, which is an
almost neutral soil, I am now growing
it in a light acid soil with a pH of 5 to
5.5, and the plant in the light acid soil
looks very much happier. In my
experience, this tuberous-rooted
plant does better in full sun than in
shade or partial shade. Propagate it
by division in spring.

Take care
Keep this species within bounds.

Take care
Give these plants a sunny spot in
which to grow. 101♦

Lobelia cardinalis

(Cardinal flower)
- **Sunny location**
- **Rich fertile moist soil**
- **Late summer flowering**

The cardinal flower is one of the most handsome herbaceous perennials. Above a rosette of green leaves, which also cover the stem, are brilliant scarlet blooms. The stems are 90cm (3ft) high.

Planting is best done in spring; initial preparation is essential, and plenty of moistened peat, leaf-mould or well-rotted garden compost should be incorporated. This species likes rich moist soil. If the ground is not forked over or cleaned for the winter, plants will come through unscathed in areas that are more or less frost-free; if doubtful, lift them in autumn and store in a dry frost-proof shed, covering the roots with peat or leaf-mould. Propagate by division in spring when the plants can be taken out of store.

Take care
Never let the roots suffer from drought during the growing season, and ensure that they have adequate moisture. 100♦

Lunaria rediviva

(Perennial honesty)
- **Partial shade**
- **Good light soil**
- **Spring flowering**

The biennial honesty, *L. annua,* is well-known and loved by flower arrangers because of its white papery seedpods, which can be used in winter flower arrangements. Seeds sown in spring will flower the following spring (ie 12 months later).

L. rediviva has four-petalled lavender to lilac fragrant flowers, which are borne on 60-90cm (2-3ft) stems above a rosette of foliage at the base. This pretty perennial honesty blooms in spring. It is to be hoped that one day it will become more popular; but it has been around since 1596. It has white papery seedpods but they are a different shape, lanceolate and tapering gradually at each end, and 8cm (3.2in) long. The leaves are larger and less serrated than those of the biennial honesty.

L. rediviva does best in half shade in good light soil. Plant it in spring, about 30cm (12in) apart. Propagate by division in spring.

Take care
Buy the perennial honesty 101♦

Lupinus polyphyllus
(Lupin)
- **Sun or light shade**
- **Light sandy loam**
- **Early summer flowering**

Lupins enjoy sun and well-drained soil; avoid lime, and heavy wet clay soils. Before planting, see that the ground is well cultivated, with an ample supply of well-rotted farmyard manure or garden compost. On well-drained soils, plant in autumn; otherwise, wait until spring.

With established plants restrict the number of flower spikes to between five and seven, when stems are about 30cm (12in) high. Give a light spraying of plain water in the evening during dry springs. As a rule staking is not necessary. Named varieties can be obtained, but the Russell hybrids have a good mixture of colours, and vary in height from 90 to 120cm (3-4ft). In very windy gardens sow the dwarf 'Lulu' lupin; this is only 60cm (24in) tall.

Propagate by basal cuttings in early spring, when 7.5-10cm (3-4in) long; insert in a cold frame.

Take care
Remove faded flowerheads to prevent them forming seeds, which will take strength from the plant. 102♦

Lychnis coronaria 'Abbotswood Rose'
(Rose campion; Dusty miller)
- **Full sun**
- **Fertile well-drained soil**
- **Summer flowering**

This species is popularly known as dusty miller because of its soft furry foliage; its leaves are coated with fine silver hairs, which almost cover the entire plant. The leaves are borne in pairs from a basal clump up the 60cm (2ft) stems on which the branching sprays of dianthus-like brilliant rose-crimson flowers of 'Abbotswood Rose' are carried (some call the flowers rose pink). It is a lovely plant, and a clump of five plants to a square metre/square yard will add charm and colour to any perennial border.

There is also a variety 'Alba', which has white flowers; apart from the colour, it is similar to the variety 'Abbotswood Rose'.

Propagate by division in autumn, but if the soil is cold and wet, leave it until spring.

Take care
These plants need a fertile soil. 102♦

Lysimachia punctata
(Loosestrife)
- **Sun or semi-shade**
- **Ordinary garden soil, preferably damp**
- **Summer flowering**

This loosestrife is quite unconnected with the purple loosestrife, *Lythrum salicaria*, but one must admit that both plants have tall and dominating flower spikes. *Lysimachia punctata* has straight stems bearing whorls of bright yellow five-petalled flowers; each stem is about 90cm (3ft) high, and it blooms for at least two months during the summer.

Plants can be invasive so it should not be grown near other perennials that could become swamped. It grows in full sun or partial shade, but although it will grow in dryish soil, it is happier where it has damp or moist soil conditions. Grouped in clumps of four plants it can give brightness to an otherwise dull corner in a garden.

Propagate by division in spring or autumn. Cuttings of young shoots can be taken in spring and inserted in sandy soil under glass. Seeds can be sown in pots or boxes in spring in a cold frame.

Take care
Do not allow these plants to crowd out weaker perennials. 103♦

Lythrum salicaria 'Firecandle'
(Purple loosestrife)
- **Sunny location**
- **Fertile moist soil**
- **Late summer flowering**

The purple loosestrife is one of the most handsome perennials during summer, when it is found growing wild on river banks, ditches and marshes. This indicates the type of soil and situation in which to grow garden varieties. But although they prefer to grow in damp boggy soil, they succeed quite happily in any moist border. The showy spikes of flowers are borne on 120cm (4ft) wiry stems. They are hardy, long lived and long flowering. The variety 'Firecandle' has deep rosy red flowers borne in the leaf axils on spikes 90cm (3ft) tall. A dwarfer one is the clear pink 'Robert', only 75cm (30in) tall. Plant bold clumps of five in the middle of the border.

Another lythrum is *L. virgatum* 'The Rocket', which is 90cm (3ft) high with erect spikes of rose-red flowers borne in the leaf axils.

Propagate by root cuttings in spring; as the rootstock is very woody division is difficult.

Take care
The ground should be moist. 104♦

Macleaya cordata

(Plume poppy)
- **Sun or light shade**
- **Rich fertile soil**
- **Late summer flowering**

This impressive and dramatic-
looking hardy herbaceous perennial
may grow to 210cm (7ft) tall. The
rough fig-like palm-shaped
sculptured glaucous foliage, silver
beneath, forms a dominating clump
from which stiff tall stems arise
displaying the small panicles of
yellow plume-like fluffy flowers
without petals. It is a plant for an
isolated bed or at the back of a large
border, for if too near the front it will
obscure any plants behind it. For a
slightly earlier display of flesh-tinted
buff flowers grow the similar *M.
microcarpa*.

The plume poppy has wandering
roots but this should not put anyone
off; if you can find a suitable part of
the border or garden, it is well worth
growing. Plant in spring. Propagate
by half-ripe cuttings in early summer,
by suckers or root cuttings in
autumn, or by division in spring.

Take care
Choose the ideal position for this
dramatic plant. 105♦

Malva moschata

(Musk mallow)
- **Sunny location**
- **Fertile and moderately well-
  drained soil**
- **Summer flowering**

This European perennial is not long
lived and in very hot weather plants
have been exhausted through heat.
The musk mallow has mid-green
finely cut buttercup-like foliage;
when bruised, this gives off a
pleasant musk-like odour, which is
more pronounced in spring. The soft
pink hollyhock-like flowers are
carried in terminal and axillary
clusters on stems about 60-75cm
(24-30in) high. The pure white *M. m.
alba* is equally charming.

Provided the soil is moderately
well drained, malvas are easily
cultivated. It pays to gather seed, so
that young stock is always available
to replace exhausted plants.
Propagate by sowing seed in spring
in sandy soil; bury them 12mm
(0.5in) deep, and place in a cold
frame. Keep moist during very hot
dry weather.

Take care
Stake if plants are in a position where
they may be windswept. 105♦

Melianthus major
(Great Cape honeyflower)
- **Sunny location**
- **Poor soil**
- **Late summer flowering**

Even though this is not a hardy
herbaceous perennial but a semi-
woody evergreen sub-shrub, its
distinct handsome alternate pinnate
leaves make it a worthwhile border
plant for gardeners near the sea or in
mild localities. The large glaucous-
green leaves, deeply serrated, have
an unpleasant smell when bruised.
Where the leaves join the main or
side stems are glaucous-green
stipules not unlike an individual
globe artichoke scale. The 'flowers'
are in fact reddish-brown bracts.
Plants can grow as high as 210cm
(7ft). This species is certainly one of
the most handsome foliage plants in
my garden.

Propagate by softwood cuttings
taken in spring and rooted in a mist
propagator, or sow seed under glass
in late summer.

Take care
Protect plants against frosts during
winter and early spring. 106♦

Mertensia virginica
(Virginian cowslip)
- **Partial shade**
- **Well-drained fertile soil**
- **Spring flowering**

This spring-flowering perennial is a
hardy plant that thrives in good
ordinary well-drained fertile soil in a
partially shady position. The tubular
flowers of cool purplish-blue
cascade in bunches among soft
blue-grey leaves, from the top of
45cm (18in) stiff stems.

During midsummer little can be
seen of this mertensia, as the stems
and foliage die down; for this reason
it is ideal for a woodland site where it
can rest until it comes into leaf and
flower the following spring. The spot
where it has flowered should be
marked. The tuberous roots are only
just under the surface, so care
should be taken not to damage them
or plants will die.

Propagate them by seed sown as
soon as ripe, or by division of the
tuberous black roots in early autumn.

Take care
Give this species partial shade, and
do not disturb it unnecessarily.

Monarda didyma 'Cambridge Scarlet'
(Bergamot; Bee balm)
- **Full sun or partial shade**
- **Moist fertile soil**
- **Summer flowering**

This fragrant perennial has nettle-like foliage. It has erect square stems, and at each joint there are pairs of pointed leaves. At its base the leaves form a dense clump. Above the several whorls of leaves, at the top of each stem, there is a crowded head of hooked scarlet flowers, also in the axil of the pairs of opposite leaves; the flowers have a pleasant fragrance.

The mat-like roots are not as a rule invasive though in well-cultivated soil they can widen, but plants are easily divided in spring, and this should be done about every third year. Today, apart from the old favourite 'Cambridge Scarlet', there are several other good varieties: 'Croftway Pink' has clear pink flowers; 'Prairie Night' is a rich violet-purple; 'Snow Maiden' is white. All are 90cm (36in) tall, except the bright ruby 'Adam', a showy variety, which is 100cm (39in).

Propagate all varieties by division in spring.

Take care
Do not let the soil dry out. 107♦

Morina longifolia
(Himalayan whorlflower)
- **Full sun**
- **Well-drained sandy loam**
- **Summer flowering**

This handsome Nepalese evergreen perennial is not seen as often as it should be. It has large slightly spiny thistle-like foliage, and leaves at the base of the stems are fragrant. The hooded tubular flowers are pink, red, yellow or white, and carried on long spikes arranged in whorls around the stout 75-90cm (30-36in) stems. Flowering starts at midsummer and goes on into early autumn.

This species needs good fertile soil, well drained but retentive, as the plant must have a certain amount of moisture. It will not tolerate cold wet soil in winter, however. Shelter should be given against spring frosts.

Propagate by sowing seed out of doors, in a well-prepared bed of rich porous soil. Apart from thinning, do not disturb the plants. The dried stems can be used by flower arrangers for winter decoration.

Take care
Protect against frost in spring.

Myrrhis odorata
(Sweet Cicely)
- **Sun or partial shade**
- **Any good soil**
- **Early summer flowering**

This old-fashioned herb is delightful
in a flower border. The 75cm (30in)
bush has mid-green fern-like foliage,
similar in flavour to sweet liquorice.
In autumn it turns a charming
burnished red, which gives another
interest in a flower border. The heads
of small creamy white flowers
brighten other plants around it; the
flowers are followed by large narrow
seedheads, first green, then black.
This is indeed a pretty and useful
hardy perennial.

 The leaves of this plant have been
used in salads and the seeds were at
one time used to scent and polish
furniture and oak floors. The plant is
also attractive to bees.

 As self-sown seedlings appear
regularly, this species is not easily
lost among other plants. The best
planting time is autumn. Propagate
by seed sown in early autumn or
spring, or by division of the carrot-
like roots in autumn or spring.

Take care
Remove unwanted self-sown
seedlings. 107♦

Nepeta × faassenii
(Catmint)
- **Sunny location**
- **Well-drained soil**
- **Early and late summer
  flowering**

Cats love nestling in a clump of
catmint. To prevent them sitting on
your plants, insert a few prickly
twigs; any cat will then soon realize
that it is no place for a nap. This plant
was for many years called *N.
mussinii.* The soft lavender-blue
flowers have a long season of bloom
from early summer to late summer,
and often into early autumn. The
flower sprays are on thin wiry grey
small-leaved stems, 45cm (18in) tall.
Nepeta makes a good edging and is
especially useful in a bed of roses.

 It is not a particularly long-lived
plant, especially on cold clay soils; it
needs a light, well-drained soil. On
heavy soil, work in sand or gritty
material around the plants. Cut the
plants back after the first flush of
flowers; this encourages more
flowers, and provides material to use
as cuttings. Plant in spring, where an
individual clump is required, putting
four plants to a square metre/square
yard. Propagate by softwood
cuttings in early to mid-summer.

Take care
Avoid winter wetness. 108♦

121

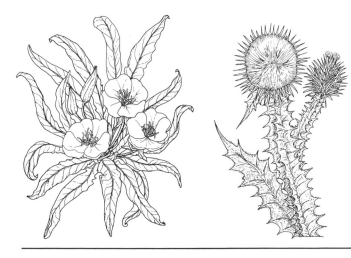

Oenothera missouriensis

(Ozark sundrops)
- **Sunny location**
- **Well-drained soil**
- **Summer and autumn flowering**

This lovely perennial ground-hugging plant, which belongs to the evening primrose family, is a native of the southern United States of America, hence its rather unusual common name, Ozark sundrops. The dark green narrow leaves lie prostrate on the ground, and above them are produced canary-yellow flowers about 7.5cm (3in) across, on 23cm (9in) reddish stems, in succession for many weeks during the summer. The flowers, which open in the evening and last for several days, are followed by equally large seedpods. Often the buds are spotted with red.

This is a superb plant for the front of a border, but to succeed it must have a well-drained soil. It is ideal for the rock garden but allow it sufficient space, because it can spread up to 60cm (24in). Propagate this species by seed in spring.

Take care
Choose a well-drained soil. 108♦

Onopordon acanthium

(Scotch thistle; Cotton thistle)
- **Sunny location**
- **Ordinary soil**
- **Summer flowering**

As the Scotch thistle is a hardy biennial, and usually found growing in a hardy flower border, it is right to include this handsome tall grey-leaved and grey-stemmed architectural plant. Both leaves and stems are covered with woolly cobweb-like hairs, and on top of its 150-210cm (5-7ft) high stems are carried purplish mauve to pale lilac thistle-like flowers.

These plants seed themselves freely, and once a plant is established the owner will never be without a plant or two in the border. Nevertheless, it is easy to eradicate any unwanted seedlings, or to give them away to friends. Position these plants at the back of the border and allow at least 90cm (3ft) for them to spread. Propagate by seeds sown out of doors in well-drained soil in spring.

Take care
Stake plants, if necessary, in windswept borders. 109♦

Ophiopogon planiscapus nigrescens

(Black-leaved lily turf)
- **Sun or partial shade**
- **Sandy well-drained soil**
- **Summer flowering**

This black-stemmed and black-leaved plant is probably of Japanese origin. The ophiopogons are related to the liriopes. It is grown for its foliage; and as it creeps slowly, it is a useful ground cover plant. The pale purple to white flowers appear in summer, and are followed by black berries. The flower stems are 15cm (6in) tall. Ophiopogon needs to be planted in front of light-leaved plants, so that the dark foliage will be more outstanding.

Not having grown this plant, I cannot write from experience, but it is said that it will grow in dry sand or (according to some authorities) in clay soils; nevertheless, my advice is to keep to well-drained soils. To be successful with ophiopogon it should be planted where it can have the benefit of shelter from a fence, wall or hedge.

Propagate this species by division in spring.

Take care
Position at the front of a border.

Osmunda regalis

(Royal fern)
- **Partial shade**
- **Moist peaty soil**
- **Early spring flowering**

This deciduous hardy perennial needs a moist peaty soil, and is best grown in half shady places, though it can be grown in full sunshine if its roots are constantly in moist soil and the plant is sheltered from cold winds. The sterile delicate pale green fronds are 120-150cm (4-5ft) long, whereas the fertile portion may be as much as 150-180cm (5-6ft). As the elegant fronds emerge from their solid clumps in spring, they look like shepherds' crooks, and in autumn they take on bright yellow and russet hues. Flower arrangers gather them, because they press and dry well.

This fern can be propagated by sowing the spores during summer, but for the amateur, propagation by division in spring is more satisfactory; the mass of black roots needs to be sliced through with a sharp spade.

Take care
The royal fern must always have its roots in moist soil. 111♦

Paeonia officinalis 'Rubra Plena'

(Old double crimson)
- **Full sun or partial shade**
- **Rich well-drained soil**
- **Late spring flowering**

'Rubra Plena' is a beautiful old peony, introduced in the sixteenth century. The large heads of double blooms are held above deeply cut foliage on stems 45-60cm (18-24in) high. Apart from 'Rubra Plena' there is the white 'Alba Plena' and the larger flowered light pink 'Rosea Superba Plena'. All three of these peonies are well worthwhile.

Peonies will grow in full sun or partial shade. Choose a site where the plants will not catch the early morning sun, as frosts can injure flower buds. When preparing the site incorporate well-rotted farmyard manure, garden compost or leaf-mould. An application of liquid manure as the buds start to swell will be beneficial. A feed of bonemeal and a mulch of humus should be worked into the soil every autumn. Propagate them by division in early autumn, or in early spring before new growth starts.

Take care
See that plants have enough moisture in dry weather. 110♦

Papaver orientale

(Oriental poppy)
- **Full sun**
- **Well-drained soil**
- **Early summer flowering**

The Oriental poppies have the largest and most flamboyant flowers of all hardy herbaceous perennials. They vary in height from 30 to 100cm (12-39in). The first colour break came in 1906 with the salmon-pink 'Mrs Perry', 90cm (36in) tall. To name only a few other varieties: 'Fireball', with double orange-scarlet flowers, 30cm (12in) tall; 'Marcus Perry', orange-scarlet, 75cm (30in); 'Perry's White', 90cm (36in); 'Curlilocks', ruffled vermilion petals, 75cm (30in); 'Black and White', white flowers with a black centre zone, 100cm (39in); and a recently introduced seedling, 'Cedric's Pink', with large greyish pink curled petals with a purple-black blotch at the base.

These poppies will thrive in full sunshine in a well-drained soil. Propagate by root cuttings in autumn or winter.

Take care
Do not let these poppies swamp less vigorous plants. 111♦

Penstemon glaber
(Blue penstemon)
- Sunny location
- Well-drained fertile soil
- Summer flowering

Having grown it recently for several years I can thoroughly recommend the blue penstemon. It has dark green glabrous strap-like leaves, 5-8cm (2-3.2in) long. Plants form thick clumps and send up flower spikes 45-60cm (18-24in) high, bearing bright blue to purple, broad-mouthed tubular flowers.

No staking is needed. Cut off the first flush of flowers and a second crop will soon take its place. One can justly call this a trouble-free hardy perennial. Even in winter the dark green foliage makes a pleasant mound in the border.

Would-be planters of this outstanding plant may need to search for it and visit several garden centres, but do persevere; it is well worth the trouble!

Propagate by taking half-ripe cuttings just below a node in late summer and inserting them in a cold frame or propagator.

Take care
Remove the first flush of flowers.

Perovskia atriplicifolia
(Russian sage)
- Sunny location
- Well-drained soil
- Late summer flowering

This is a sub-shrubby deciduous hardy perennial, though more often than not it is grown in herbaceous borders rather than among shrubs. The whole plant has a sage-like odour, especially when it is brushed against. It has coarsely toothed grey-green foliage, and a profusion of soft lavender-blue flowers during late summer. A variety worth growing is 'Blue Spire', with deeply cut leaves and larger lavender-blue flowers.

This species needs to be grown in full sun, in well-drained loamy soil. An annual pruning should be given just as buds start to break in spring; cut all shoots hard back to the base, leaving perhaps two buds to develop on each. The plant will then send up new shoots 90-150cm (3-5ft) high. Propagate by cuttings of half-ripe shoots in midsummer, inserted in sandy cuttings mixture in a propagating frame.

Take care
Give this plant plenty of room.

'Vintage Wine'

Phlomis russeliana

(Jerusalem sage)
- Sunny location
- Well-drained ordinary soil
- Summer flowering

The Jerusalem sage is also found
under other specific names: one is *P.
samia,* which is frequently used by
nurserymen, and another is *P.
viscosa.* But, for our purposes, *P.
russeliana* is its name. This
handsome weed-smothering plant,
or ground coverer, has large rough
puckered heart-shaped felty sage-
like grey-green leaves. Among the
foliage stout flower spikes, 75-90cm
(30-36in) high, carry whorls of soft
rich yellow hooded flowers in early to
mid-summer. The attractive
seedheads can be used successfully
in flower arrangements, whether
green or dried. Phlomis will grow in
ordinary garden soil in an open,
sunny location.

Propagation of this plant is by
seed, cuttings or division, in spring
or autumn.

Take care
Plant phlomis against a suitable
background, such as a red-leaved
Japanese maple. 112♦

Phlox paniculata

(Phlox)
- Sun or light shade
- Light fertile soil
- Summer to late summer
  flowering

Although many amateurs favour
common or popular names, as far as
I know phlox are simply phlox. The
species *P. paniculata* is the ancestor
from which all the colourful named
varieties have sprung. Their brilliant
and quiet colours and wonderful
musky fragrance can never be
forgotten. The times of day to enjoy
phlox to perfection are daybreak or
sunset.

Many older varieties are no longer
easily available, but there is still a
good selection of varieties and
colours. The purple-red 'Vintage
Wine' has huge trusses, on 75cm
(30in) stems; 'Windsor' is clear
carmine with a magenta eye, 110cm
(44in) tall; the strong 'Border Gem' is
cyclamen-purple with a peony-
purple eye, 90cm (36in) tall; 'Mother
of Pearl' has pretty pink trusses and
is 75cm (30in) tall; the dark-foliaged
blue 'Hampton Court' is of similar
height; and for a variegated variety
there is 'Harlequin' bearing rich
purple flowers, 90cm (36in) tall.
'Prince of Orange' is a stunning
orange-salmon colour, also 90cm
(36in) high; the pure white Fujuyana

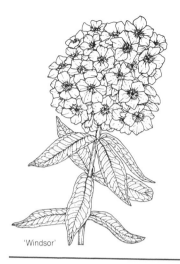

'Windsor'

Phuopsis stylosa
(Crosswort; Foetid crucinella)
- **Full sun**
- **Sandy or chalky soils**
- **Summer flowering**

from the USA has magnificent cylindrical trusses and is 75cm (30in) tall; two 90cm (36in) beauties are the pale lilac 'Prospero' and the deep crimson 'Red Indian'. For a pure white choose 'White Admiral', 75cm (30in) high; and for a real dwarf the 45cm (18in) 'Pinafore Pink', a charming variety with large trusses of bright pink.

Phlox are best in a light soil with a good supply of humus, well-rotted farmyard manure or well-rotted garden compost, and – in very dry weather – sufficient moisture for their needs. What they do not like is chalk or clay soils. Gritty or gravelly soils are satisfactory, provided there is enough humus and the soil is never allowed to dry out.

Only one pest attacks phlox, that is the eelworm. To avoid it, propagate plants from root cuttings, in autumn or winter.

This little mat-forming gem from Persia and the Caucasus was for many years known as *Crucinella stylosa,* but now its genus is *Phuopsis.* It gets its common name foetid crucinella because of its fox-like musky odour, though personally I have never found it objectionable. The 25-30cm (10-12in) stems are clothed in small slender foliage; on these stems are borne pretty little tubular flowers that form a crosswise design, hence its other common name, crosswort. The bright rosy-pink flower clusters make an attractive display throughout the summer. It is a first-rate plant for the front of the border or as an edging plant to a path. There are other coloured forms with scarlet and purple flowers.

Propagate crosswort by sowing seeds in the open ground in spring, or by division of the roots in early autumn.

Take care
Do not let phlox dry out in very hot dry summers. 129♦

Take care
This plant likes plenty of sun. 130♦

Phygelius capensis

(Cape figwort)
- **Sunny location**
- **Well-drained fertile soil**
- **Summer and autumn flowering**

In its native habitat this South African beauty is a shrub, but it is equally happy growing as a hardy perennial. The flowers are not unlike those of a fuchsia. The opposite leaves are attached to stiff stalks which carry the candelabra-like tubular flowers, which are crimson-scarlet with yellow throats. The flowers hang down like trumpets, enhanced by the protruding stamens.

Where plants are growing in maritime districts or are trained to a sunny sheltered wall, they can be grown as shrubby perennials. Plants trained against a wall can reach 180cm (6ft) or more. In more exposed gardens, plants may become badly damaged by frost; when this happens cut them back to encourage new growth and healthy shoots in spring.

Propagate this species by half-ripe cuttings in summer or by seed sown in gentle heat in spring.

Take care
Protect plants in unsheltered areas or frost pockets.

Physostegia virginiana

(Obedient plant)
- **Sun or partial shade**
- **Any good fertile soil**
- **Late summer flowering**

This hardy herbaceous perennial is well named the obedient plant, because its flowers have hinged stalks and can be moved from side to side and remain as altered on their square stems. The long narrow dark green glossy leaves are toothed and grow in four columns; the dull rose-pink flowers terminate the square tapering spikes, 45-105cm (18-42in) tall. They bloom from summer to autumn, until the frosts spoil their beauty. Physostegia has vigorous stoloniferous rootstocks that spread underground.

There are several good varieties: 'Rose Bouquet' has pinkish mauve trumpet flowers; 'Summer Snow', pure white, is about 75cm (30in) high; and 'Vivid' bears rose-crimson flowers on stalks 30-45cm (12-18in) tall.

Propagate by division in spring, or by root cuttings in winter.

Take care
Give this plant sufficient moisture during dry summer weather. 131♦

Above: **Phlox paniculata**
'Vintage Wine'
This purple-red variety has fairly
compact flower trusses that are
freely produced on stems 75cm
(30in) tall. Beautifully fragrant. 126-7▸

Above: **Physostegia virginiana 'Rose Bouquet'**
Spires of tubular pink-mauve flowers up to 60cm (24in) long are carried above the large, coarsely toothed leaves during late summer. 128▸

Right:
Physostegia virginiana 'Alba'
One of the attractive white varieties of this hardy perennial. Grow these plants in fertile soil and water well during hot dry weather. 128▸

Left: **Phuopsis stylosa**
A mat-forming plant ideal for the front of the border or for edging a path. It thrives in bright sun, producing its delightful rosy pink flowers throughout the summer. 127▸

Left: **Polemonium foliosissimum**
*Rich lavender-blue flowers on stems
75cm (30in) high grace this hardy
perennial during the summer. Grow
in deep fertile soil.* 145♦

Below left:
Polygonatum × hybridum
*This adaptable hardy perennial bears
arching stems of sweetly scented
bell-shaped flowers in spring.* 145♦

Right: **Polygonum amplexicaule
'Atrosanguineum'**
*Crimson flower spikes are freely
produced by this vigorous perennial
from summer into the autumn.* 146♦

Below: **Potentilla atrosanguinea
'Gibson's Scarlet'**
*Stunning single red flowers are
produced on 30cm (12in) stems
above strawberry-like foliage.* 146♦

Above: **Rudbeckia fulgida 'Goldsturm'**
These bright flowers are superb for cutting from late summer. 149♦

Below: **Ranunculus aconitifolius 'Flore Pleno'**
Attractive double button-like blooms on stems up to 60cm (24in) tall. 148♦

Above: **Salvia superba**
This is a hardy and adaptable plant
that will thrive in any soil. It produces
abundant spikes of lovely violet-
purple flowers over a long period
from early summer. 149♦

Above:
Sedum spectabile 'Autumn Joy'
Easy to grow and spectacular in bloom, the ice plants are to be recommended. This variety has rose flowers changing to salmon pink. 152♦

Left: **Saponaria officinalis**
This is the original single-flowered form, with fragrant rose-pink blooms carried on erect stems up to 90cm (3ft) in height. Double-flowered forms are also available. 150♦

Right: **Schizostylis coccinea 'Major'**
In warm moist surroundings this plant will thrive in most types of soil and produce these stunning star-shaped flowers in autumn. 151♦

Above: **Sidalcea malvaeflora**
*Lovely flowers in varying shades of
pink are borne on stems up to 135cm
(4.5ft) tall depending on variety. Cut
down after flowering to encourage
lateral shoots to develop.* 153♦

Left: **Sisyrinchium striatum
'Variegatum'**
*Slender stems with yellowish-white
flowers grow to a height of about
90cm (3ft) in summer; the foliage
remains through the winter.* 153♦

Right: **Solidago 'Goldenmosa'**
*This superb variety grows to about
75cm (30in) in height with lovely
frothy yellow flowers in late summer.
It will grow vigorously in any good
soil, in sun or partial shade.* 154♦

Above:
Thalictrum speciosissimum
This plant is much prized by flower *arrangers, particularly for its long-lasting glaucous foliage. Yellow flowers are borne in summer.* 155♦

Above: **Stachys olympica 'Silver Carpet'**
An excellent ground cover plant that does not produce flowers. 155♦

Below:
Tradescantia virginiana 'Isis'
The striking purple-blue flowers are long-lasting in summer. 156♦

Left: **Trollius × cultorum 'Fire Globe'**
This is a plant that will thrive in a moist situation, next to a pond for example. It flowers in the spring at a height of 75cm (30in). 156♦

Right: **Veronica spicata**
Plant these at the front of a sunny border and they will provide a colourful display in summer. This is the original species; the varieties offer other colours. 157♦

Below: **Tropaeolum speciosum**
Bright scarlet flowers appear on the twining stems of this attractive plant throughout the summer months. An excellent subject for growing over an evergreen shrub. 157♦

Above: **Zantedeschia aethiopica 'Crowborough'**
This fairly hardy arum lily will grow in an open border or in moist ground next to a pond or stream. White spathes appear in summer. 158♦

Polemonium foliosissimum

(Jacob's ladder)
- Sunny location
- Deep rich fertile soil
- Early to late summer flowering

The polemonium has been known since Roman times, and its generic name is after King Polemon of Pontus. Most gardeners know *P. caeruleum*, which seeds so freely. *P. foliosissimum* (a mouthful of a name) is the longest-lived of these pretty hardy perennials. It has pinnate foliage bearing clusters of pretty five-petalled lavender-blue flowers, enriched by orange-yellow stamens, and massed together on upright 75cm (30in) stems from early to late summer. There is also an earlier flowering variety called 'Sapphire', which has light blue flowers on 45cm (18in) stems and is equally long lived.

   Grow polemoniums in a rich fertile soil for a fine display of flowers. Propagate these plants by division in early autumn or spring.

Take care
Buy plants of the long-lived *P. foliosissimum*, as it hardly ever produces seed. 132♦

Polygonatum × hybridum

(Solomon's seal)
- Sun or shade
- Fertile retentive soil
- Late spring flowering

This is a most graceful hardy herbaceous perennial, with fat rhizomatous roots that need to be grown in groups. The 90cm (36in) stems, which have a pretty arching habit, are clothed with stalkless alternate broad ribbed lance-like fresh green foliage. On the opposite side to each leaf, pretty little greenish white fragrant bells hang down from horizontal arching stems. Gather stems when the flowers are in bud and take them indoors; when they open they will fill a room with their scent.

   The rhizomes should be just below soil level. Solomon's seal is happiest in a retentive soil well endowed with leaf-mould or well-rotted garden compost. Propagate it by division in autumn or spring.

   Foliage can be skeletonized by the Solomon's seal sawfly. At the first sign of a holed leaf, spray or dust at once with malathion.

Take care
Keep moist when growing in full sun during very dry weather. 132♦

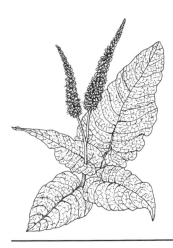

Polygonum amplexicaule 'Atrosanguineum'
(Mountain fleece-flower)
- Sun or partial shade
- Good moist soil
- Summer to autumn flowering

A polygonum that is a must for any flower border. This attractive hardy herbaceous perennial has a woody rootstock, from which arise erect 105-120cm (42-48in) flower stems clothed in heart-shaped foliage, with an abundance of tiny rosy crimson flowerings forming spikes up to 15cm (6in) long at the end of each shoot during summer and into autumn. Plants form a large leafy clump, increasing in size every year. Grow at least four plants together, as one on its own does not make much of a show. Provide rich moist soil for best results and grow in sun or semi-shade.

Propagate this polygonum by seed sown in a cool house or frame in spring, or by division of roots in spring, which is the more satisfactory method.

Take care
Keep moist; if they become dry at the roots, flowering will be poor. 133♦

Potentilla atrosanguinea
(Himalayan cinquefoil)
- Full sun
- Fertile well-drained soil
- Early and late summer flowering

The best-known variety of *P. atrosanguinea* is 'Gibson's Scarlet', which has brilliant single red flowers on 30cm (12in) stems from mid- to late summer. Larger-flowered varieties include the double orange-flame 'William Rollison', also the double mahogany-coloured 'Monsieur Rouillard'; and the grey-foliaged 'Gloire de Nancy', which has semi-double orange-crimson flowers almost 5cm (2in) across, on 45cm (18in) branching stems; all bloom from early to late summer.

The potentillas, with strawberry-like foliage, are best in full sun, but can tolerate partial shade. They enjoy good well-drained soil, but if the soil is too rich it results in extra lush foliage at the expense of the flowers. Avoid growing potentillas in moist or stagnant ground in winter.

Propagate by division in spring or autumn.

Take care
These potentillas sprawl, so give ample space; plant in groups. 133♦

Primula denticulata
(Drumstick primrose)
- **Partial shade**
- **Cool rich retentive soil**
- **Spring flowering**

In spring this Himalayan primula produces dense globular heads of fragrant flowers of pale lavender, mauve, lilac, lilac-purple, rich carmine or deepest purple, on stout olive-green stalks about 30cm (12in) high. There is also an attractive white form, *P. denticulata alba.* The erect stalks are lightly covered with a powdered meal, as is the pale green foliage, which forms large tufts at the base of each plant.

Although this perennial is perfectly hardy, early sharp frosts can sometimes slightly damage the foliage; if a sheltered place can be found, damage is less likely to happen. The drumstick primroses, when grown in a sunny border, need moisture throughout the summer, or a deep moist rich soil. Propagate them from seeds sown as soon as ripe in summer in a shady spot. To keep forms true to colour, increase by root cuttings in winter.

Take care
Choose a semi-shady position.

Pulmonaria officinalis
(Lungwort; Soldiers and sailors)
- **Full or partial shade**
- **Any good fertile soil**
- **Spring flowering**

This early flowering perennial is so called because its spotted leaves are said to resemble (and were once thought to cure) diseased lungs. The flowers of *P. officinalis,* carried on 25cm (10in) stems, are bright pink when first open, turning later to a purplish-blue; the large leaves are spotted with white. *P. saccharata* has longer and narrower leaves, almost grey and moderately spotted, and its pink and blue tubular flowers are carried on 30cm (12in) stems. *P. officinalis* and *P. saccharata* are more or less evergreen, but one that almost dies down in late autumn and winter is *P. angustifolia* 'Munstead Blue' or 'Munstead Variety'; the 15cm (6in) stems emerge with clusters of pretty pinkish purple buds in late winter, and the blue tubular flowers appear in early spring.

Divide plants in autumn or spring.

Take care
Do not plant pulmonarias too near to trees when in full shade; the tree roots can rob the soil of moisture.

Pyrethrum roseum
(Chrysanthemum coccineum)
(Pyrethrum)
- **Sunny location**
- **Good fertile soil**
- **Early summer flowering**

Many fine varieties of pyrethrums have been introduced and named, both single and double forms. 'Eileen May Robinson' a large single pale rose-pink variety, has erect stout stems that are 80cm (32in) tall, with flowers 7.5cm (3in) across. Pyrethrum 'Brenda' is also single, with Tyrian purple flowers 9.5cm (3.75in) across on erect 90cm (3ft) stems. For a double, choose the large-flowered pink 'Progression', 90cm (3ft) tall, or the pure white double 'Aphrodite', of perfect shape, 60-70cm (24-28in) high. All these varieties are excellent as cut flowers.

Propagate pyrethrums by division in early autumn or early spring, doing this every second year. They will thrive in a fertile well-drained soil in an open, sunny position.

Ranunculus aconitifolius 'Flore Pleno'
(Fair maids of France)
- **Sun or partial shade**
- **Well-drained soil**
- **Late spring flowering**

The common name conjures up in one's mind that here is a plant which must be delicately lovely and it is. The double-flowered 'Flore Pleno' has dark green deeply cut buttercup-like foliage, and on 60cm (24in) stems it bears delightful sprays of perfect pure white buttons, those elegant 'fair maids of France'. These flowers are about 1.25cm (0.5in) across and appear during the early summer months. It is a fine plant where it will flourish.

Provided this ranunculus has good fertile soil and is not allowed to become dry, the little beauty should be no bother. In a sheltered position it will grow equally well in sunshine or partial shade. Propagate it by division, either in spring or immediately after flowering.

Take care
Support with twiggy peasticks, from early in the season.

Take care
Do not let the soil dry out during hot dry weather. 134♦

Rudbeckia fulgida
(Black-eyed Susan)
- **Full sun**
- **Moist fertile soil**
- **Late summer and autumn flowering**

This species has also been known as *R. speciosa* and *R. newmanii*; but whatever one calls it, it is one of the most useful border and cut flowers in late summer and autumn. Erect 60cm (24in) stems rise from leafy clumps, displaying several large golden-yellow daisy-like flowers with short blackish-purple central discs or cones, hence the name black-eyed Susan. The narrow leaves are rather rough to handle. Other garden forms of *R. fulgida* are the free-flowering *deamii,* 90cm (36in) tall, and 'Goldsturm', which above its bushy growth has stems 60cm (24in) tall carrying chrome-yellow flowers with dark brown cones. Rudbeckias make good cut flowers and blend very well with *Aster amellus* 'King George'.

Propagate by dividing the plants, in autumn or spring.

Take care
Do not let these dry out during the summer. 134♦

Salvia superba
(Long-branched sage)
- **Sun or partial shade**
- **Any good fertile soil**
- **Early summer to late autumn flowering**

For many years this plant was known as *S. virgata nemerosa*. Each erect 90cm (36in) stem carries branching spikes of violet-purple flowers, with reddish-brown bracts (ie modified leaves). Today there are also dwarf varieties, such as 'Lubeca', with masses of spikes of violet-blue flowers, 75cm (30in) high; and 'East Friesland', violet-purple, and only 45cm (18in) tall. These salvias look well when planted on their own.

Salvias are both fully hardy and perennial, and will grow in any good fertile soil or on chalk, but they dislike dry soils, and should not be allowed to dry out. Some form of support should be given, such as peasticks pushed in around the plants to allow them to grow through. Propagate salvias by division in spring or autumn.

Take care
Support the tall varieties. 135♦

Saponaria officinalis
(Bouncing bet; Soapwort)
- **Sunny location**
- **Well-drained soil**
- **Summer to early autumn
  flowering**

This plant is called soapwort
because a lather can be made from
the foliage and used for cleaning old
curtains. This wilding can be seen in
hedgerows in summer and early
autumn. It is a handsome perennial,
but its roots can spread beneath the
ground. It has panicles of large
fragrant rose-pink flowers, 2.5-3cm
(1-1.2in) across, carried on terminal
loose heads on erect 60-90cm (24-
36in) stems. The three-veined
leaves are 5-13cm (2-5in) long and
5cm (2in) wide. Double forms are
'Roseo Plena', which is pink, and the
white 'Albo Plena'.

   All do well in good well-drained
soil, but lime or chalk soils should be
avoided. Propagate by half-ripe
cuttings in summer, or by division in
spring.

Take care
These plants can spread and
become untidy, but do not exclude
them from your garden on this
account. 136♦

Saxifraga fortunei
(Fortune's saxifrage)
- **Shady location**
- **Rich fertile soil**
- **Autumn flowering**

Even though it is 120 years since this
saxifrage was introduced from China
by Robert Fortune, it is still not freely
planted. It flowers in autumn, and
into early winter in some years.
Above the glossy fleshy bright green
foliage, which is reddish beneath,
are the delicate sprays of pure white,
unevenly rayed star-shaped flowers
carried on fleshy branching 30-45cm
(12-18in) stems. It makes a useful
cut flower in autumn.

   This species needs a cool shady
situation in rich soil, preferably one
offering some degree of shelter.
Saxifraga fortunei 'Wada's Form' has
purplish leaves which are crimson
beneath.

   Propagate by division of the plant,
either in spring or immediately after
flowering has finished.

Take care
Plant in a cool shaded spot such as
the edge of a woodland border.

Saxifraga × urbium
(London pride)
● **Full sun or partial shade**
● **Any ordinary soil**
● **Late spring to early summer flowering**

London Pride is one of those charming plants that should be grown in every garden. It is named not after the City of London, but after George London, a partner in an 18th century nursery firm. No doubt if *S. × urbium* (once known as *S. × umbrosa*) was difficult to grow it would be more appreciated. This evergreen perennial has rosettes of oblong slightly fleshy leaves with slender 30cm (12in) needle-like stems that carry sprays of star-shaped flowers, pinkish white and freely dotted with delicate red spots. There are also variegated forms such as *S. × urbium* 'Variegata' and *S. × u.* 'Variegata Aurea' with pretty yellow spots.

The variegated forms must be grown in full sunshine or they will lose their markings. They will need moisture in summer, and an annual mulch of humus. Propagate by division in autumn or spring.

Take care
Plant in partial shade if possible, except variegated forms.

Schizostylis coccinea
(Kaffir lily)
● **Full sun**
● **Any moist fertile soil**
● **Early autumn flowering**

This S African relative of the irises appears to grow and flower freely in most soils. In South Africa it grows near water, and it needs ample moisture to flower. It has long stems, 60-75cm (24-30in) or more; pretty cup-shaped flowers open in a star-like fashion, not unlike small gladiolus flowers. *S. coccinea* has rich crimson blooms about 4cm (1.6in) across; 'Major' and 'Gigantea' are even brighter and larger, 'Mrs Hegarty' is pale pink, and 'Sunrise' has large pink flowers. The flowering stems are excellent for cutting.

The rhizomatous roots need to be lifted, divided and replanted every few years to keep them thriving. A spring mulch of peat or well-rotted garden compost will help to retain moisture around the plants. Propagate by division in spring, always leaving four to six shoots on each portion.

Take care
Be sure to keep them moist. 137♦

Scrophularia aquatica 'Variegata'

(Variegated figwort)
- **Partial shade**
- **Moist soil**
- **Spring to autumn**

An evergreen hardy perennial grown for its variegated foliage; the leaves are prettily striped, with creamy markings. Its insignificant flowers are best removed, to encourage better-marked and stronger foliage and also to prevent self-sown seedlings popping up where not wanted. The rigid upright 60cm (24in) stems are clothed with opposite leaves from spring to autumn.

It is happiest growing in semi-shade, as in full sun the foliage may become dry and lose some of its lovely markings. The old stems can be cut back in early winter when they look untidy. Propagate by dividing and replanting during the spring. Alternatively, take almost ripe cuttings in the autumn and insert them in sandy soil in a cold frame.

Take care
Provide ample moisture during summer months.

Sedum spectabile 'Autumn Joy'

(Ice plant)
- **Full sun**
- **Well-drained soil**
- **Late summer/autumn flowering**

The name ice plant probably originated because this species has glaucous glistening foliage. The leaves are opposite or in threes, and clasp stout erect stems 30-60cm (12-24in) high. Above these stems are borne flat plate-like unbranched flowers. *S. spectabile* has pale pink blooms. The varieties 'Carmen' and 'Meteor' are a deeper pink, and 'Brilliant' is a deep rose pink. 'Autumn Joy' is at first pale rose, gradually changing to a beautiful salmon pink; later it turns a beautiful brown to give a pleasant winter display. The flat flowerheads will be besieged by bees.

These sedums can be grown with the minimum of attention. Propagate them by taking stem cuttings in midsummer, and rooting in sandy soil in a cold frame, or by division in late summer or autumn.

Take care
Give these sedums room – about five plants to a square metre. 137♦

Sidalcea malvaeflora
(Greek mallow; Prairie mallow)
- **Full sun**
- **Good ordinary soil**
- **Summer flowering**

These mallow-flowered beauties are most graceful perennials. The funnel-shaped flowers in varying shades of pink are carried in terminal branching spikes on stout stems 120-135cm (4-4.5ft) high. The leaves are divided like a hand. Varieties to choose from include: 'Croftway Red', a deep rich red, 90cm (3ft) tall; 'Rose Queen', deep rosy pink, 120cm (4ft); 'William Smith', salmon-pink, 105cm (42in); and 'Sussex Beauty', a clear satiny rose-pink, 90cm (3ft).

They may be attacked by hollyhock rust, but there is no need to worry. Propagate them by division, in autumn or spring. Support the taller varieties with canes and cut down plants after flowering to encourage the development of lateral shoots to flower the following season.

Take care
If hollyhock rust attacks, spray the plants with zineb. 138♦

Sisyrinchium striatum
(Satin flower)
- **Sunny location**
- **Well-drained soil**
- **Summer flowering**

This Chilean species is liked by some, but bitterly disliked by others. It is evergreen, and it gives grey-green sword-like foliage throughout the year. In winter its 45-60cm (18-24in) iris-like foliage makes a handsome fan in the borders, and in summer the 75-90cm (30-36in) rigid slender stems are closely packed with many pale yellowish-white flowers; the reverse of the petals is striped with purple. The flowers are carried on about half the total length of the stems. Grow it in a sunny place in well-drained soil with added leaf-mould or peat.

After a year or so plants suddenly die, but it seeds itself freely. It is a good idea to cut down the faded flower stems and any dead leaves during the autumn. Propagate it by division in autumn.

Take care
Transplant self-sown seedlings to form a tidy clump. 138♦

Smilacina racemosa
(False Solomon's seal)
● **Shade**
● **Moist rich soil**
● **Spring flowering**

Smilacina enjoys similar conditions to lily of the valley. Its slender pointed fresh green spear-like leaves are downy beneath, and stick out right and left alternately from the stem. The little trusses of creamy-white scented frothy flowers are also arranged alternately, and are distributed on the underside of the arching 75cm (30in) stems. In autumn the flowers are followed by red berries.

 Provided it is given shade and moisture, and no lime, this species will not be any bother. It must not be allowed to dry out during summer; therefore if at all possible choose a site where it will have shade and moisture at its roots. Propagate by division of the rhizomatous roots in autumn. Do not divide in the first year after planting; the roots spread slowly underground and should not be disturbed until the plant is fully established.

Take care
Do not let the roots dry out.

Solidago 'Goldenmosa'
(Aaron's rod; Golden rod)
● **Sun or partial shade**
● **Good ordinary soil**
● **Late summer flowering**

Golden rod, at one time, meant some small yellow one-sided sprays at the top of tall stout hairy stems. Today, there is a much larger selection. The variety 'Goldenmosa' has pretty frothy flowers, miniature heads of the original golden rod, similar to mimosa; the rough hairy flower spikes are 75cm (30in) tall. Two smaller varieties are the 45cm (18in) 'Cloth of Gold', with deep yellow flowers, and 'Golden Thumb', with clear yellow flowers on 30cm (12in) stems, which produces neat little bushes ideal for the front of the border.

 These vigorous plants will thrive in any good soil well supplied with nutrients. A sunny location or one in partial shade will suit them equally well. Propagate them all by division in spring.

Take care
Apply humus to taller varieties. 139♦

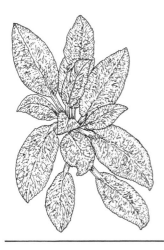 

Stachys olympica 'Silver Carpet'

(Lamb's ear; Lamb's tongue)
● **Full sun**
● **Well-drained soil**
● **Non-flowering**

S. olympica (once *S. lanata*) flowers very freely, but 'Silver Carpet' is a non-flowering variety. It makes excellent ground cover and does not have the disadvantage of producing flower stems, which look untidy once the plant has finished flowering. If you have *S. olympica,* cut off the flowerheads as soon as they are over. Both *S. olympica* and 'Silver Carpet' are evergreen.

A quite different stachys is *S. macrantha* (syn. *S. grandiflora*), or big betony. This has heart-shaped hairy white foliage which is a soft green and very wrinkled. The rosy-violet flowers are held on erect stems 30cm (12in) high. Varieties of this include 'Robusta', 60cm (24in) high, with large violet-mauve flowers, and the rosy pink 'Rosea Superba'. They flower during summer.

Propagate stachys by division, in spring or autumn.

Take care
Do not let these encroach on other perennials. 141♦

Thalictrum speciosissimum

(Dusty meadow rue)
● **Sun or light shade**
● **Any good fertile soil**
● **Summer flowering**

Some meadow rues are much sought after by flower arrangers for their foliage. *T. speciosissimum* (also known as *T. flavum glaucum*) has lovely glaucous leaves pinnately cut and divided. The foliage lasts longer than the frothy pale yellow flowers carried on huge panicles at the top of stout 150cm (5ft) stems. This is a back of the border perennial, or on its own if grown for cutting.

T. delavayi (generally known as *T. dipterocarpum*) is another lovely meadow rue, with branching panicles of rosy mauve flowers with bright yellow stamens. It needs rich well-cultivated soil, and staking if planted in a windy site. The form 'Hewitt's Double' has rich mauve flowers.

Propagate by division in spring, and 'Hewitt's Double' by offsets also in spring.

Take care
Obtain the correct plant when buying these thalictrums. 140♦

Tradescantia virginiana 'Isis'

(Spiderwort)

- **Sun or partial shade**
- **Any good fertile soil**
- **Summer and autumn flowering**

The spiderworts are probably better known as house plants, but the hardy herbaceous perennials are much larger. *T. virginiana* has a number of varieties from which to choose. These perennials have smooth almost glossy curving strap-shaped leaves, ending in a cradle-like effect, where a continuous display of three-petalled flowers emerges throughout summer and autumn.

The variety 'Isis' has deep blue flowers and is 45cm (18in) high. The pure white 'Osprey', has three-petalled crested flowers, and another pure white of similar height is 'Innocence'. Two 50cm (20in) varieties are the carmine-purple 'Purewell Giant' and the rich velvety 'Purple Dome'.

Plant them in clumps, not singly; on their own they are not effective, but clumps make a splash of colour. Propagate them by division in spring or autumn.

Trollius × cultorum

(Globe flower)

- **Sun or dappled shade**
- **Moist soil**
- **Spring flowering**

Globe flowers thrive best in moist soil, and they need plenty of humus such as leaf-mould, well-rotted farmyard manure or good garden compost, especially in drier ground.

The following varieties are worth considering 'Fire Globe' is 75cm (30in) tall, with deeply cut large dark green foliage and rich orange-yellow globular flowers; of similar height, 'Goldquelle' is a vigorous plant with pale buttercup-yellow globular flowers; 'Canary Bird' is not quite 60cm (24in) high, with coarsely divided dark green foliage and large cup-shaped bright golden-yellow flowers. If your soil does not dry out, plant 45cm (18in) 'Earliest of All', with medium-size foliage, and bright golden-yellow, cup-shaped flowers in early spring.

Propagate all varieties by division in spring.

Take care
Plant near the front of a border. 141♦

Take care
Keep moist in summer. 142♦

Tropaeolum speciosum

(Scotch flame flower)
- **Shade and sun**
- **Retentive moist soil**
- **Summer and autumn flowering**

This beautiful perennial can be bitterly disappointing, because its fleshy roots are difficult to establish. Once settled it is a joy. Pretty six-lobed leaves are carried on twining stems that are best seen rambling over evergreen shrubs or hedges. From midsummer through to the autumn the plant is covered with superb scarlet flowers about 4cm (1.6in) across and with attractive spurs. The plant is best suited to cool moist country gardens; it is not ideal for towns and cities.

The warm ochre-yellow flowers of *T. polyphyllum* are equally lovely, but it prefers its fleshy roots in well-drained hot sunny positions.

Propagate by seed sown in spring in a cold frame, or by division in spring.

Veronica spicata

(Spiked speedwell)
- **Full sun**
- **Good ordinary soil**
- **Summer flowering**

"border blue" must dead head

Provided these cultivated speedwells have reasonably good soil and are grown in a sunny position near the front of the border, the result will be very pleasing. The rich rose pink spikes of 'Barcarolle' form above a deep green mat on 30-45cm (12-18in) stems. The light pink 'Minuet' is of a similar height but has grey-green foliage. Two recent varieties are 'Blue Fox', with bright lavender-blue flowers on 30-40cm (12-16in) spikes, and the long-flowering deep-coloured 'Red Fox' with 35cm (14in) erect stems.

A late summer flowering Australian species is *V. perfoliata,* the Digger's speedwell. It has grey glaucous leaves, and the 60cm (24in) stems carry sprays of Spode-blue flowers.

Propagate all these speedwells by division in autumn or spring.

Take care
Be patient. 142-3♦

Take care
Plant near the front of the border. 143♦

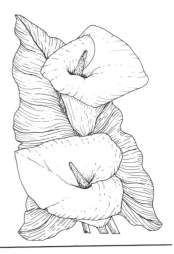

Viscaria vulgaris 'Splendens Plena'

(German catchfly)
- **Sunny location**
- **Fertile moderately drained soil**
- **Early summer flowering**

For many years this species was called *Lychnis viscaria*, but now it is *Viscaria vulgaris*. The branching 45cm (18in) stems of 'Splendens Plena' bear sprays of double cerise flowers in early summer. At the base of each plant is a tuft of narrow dark green grass-like foliage. All parts of the German catchfly are sticky, which gives the plant its common name. The white variety, 'Alba', has lighter green foliage; its single white flowers are shaded cool green, and carried on 23cm (9in) stalks. The single *V. vulgaris* has carmine-pink flowers on 25cm (10in) stalks.

All three are excellent as border edging. When planted as a clump, five or six plants are needed for each square metre/yard. Propagate them by seed sown out of doors in spring, or by division of plants in autumn or spring.

Take care
Divide and replant every third or fourth year.

Zantedeschia aethiopica 'Crowborough'

(Hardy arum lily)
- **Sunny location**
- **Dry or wet soil**
- **Summer flowering**

This is a hardy arum lily, but during its first few years after planting some form of protection should be given. This hardy variety is about 90cm (3ft) high and has white fleshy spathes with spear-shaped foliage. The bright yellow 'true' flowers are borne on a fleshy spadix enclosed by the large white spathe, which is a modified bract.

In future years, once the plants are established, give a good thick mulch of leaf-mould or bracken. When planting, place the roots about 10cm (4in) below soil level; as plants mature it will be found that the roots will penetrate more deeply. 'Crowborough' will put up with dry as well as moist conditions, and will flourish in heavy soil.

Propagate in late spring, by removing young offsets at the base of the plants.

Take care
Protect newly planted stock. 144▶

Index of Common Names

Credits

Line artwork
The drawings in this book have been prepared by Maureen Holt
© Salamander Books Ltd.

Photographs
The majority of the photographs in this book have been taken by Eric Crichton. © Salamander Books Ltd.

Copyright in the following photographs belong to the suppliers:

Pat Brindley: 105(B), 106, 107(B), 108(B), 109.

Erich Crichton: 33, 35(B), 38(B), 41, 46(B), 47, 48, 65, 68-9(T), 72(T), 76(B), 78(T), 80, 98(B), 101(B), 102-3(T), 103(B), 110, 111, 112, 135, 138(B), 140, 142(T), 144.

Noël Prockter: 134(B)

Editorial assistance
Copy-editing and proof-reading: Maureen Cartwright.